John Bowen & Sons
Builders and Edwardi 187(

Anthony Collins

ISBN 978-0-9930538-1-8
© Anthony Collins, 2020.

Published by
Anthony Collins Publishing
134 Edmund Street
Birmingham B3 2ES

Designed and printed by
Adlard Print & Reprographics
Ruddington, Nottingham
www.adlardprint.com

The illustration of the cover page is of an Aveling & Porter roller with employees of John Bowen & Sons, whilst building Netherne Hospital in Surrey between the years 1905 - 1910.

The dark lake colour of the cover of this book reflects the livery of the company.

All possible care has been taken in tracing the ownership of any copyright material used in this book and in making acknowledgement for its use. If any owner has not been acknowledged, the author and the publishers will be glad of the opportunity to rectify the error.

Introduction

In 2014 I published a book on the life of my great grandfather entitled 'Alderman John Bowen J.P'. Known as 'Honest John', John Bowen was reputed to have walked into Birmingham in 1870 as a carpenter at the age of 26 and shortly afterwards founded the building firm that became John Bowen & Sons.

Unfortunately, no records of the firm survive and apart from the obituaries of John Bowen published in the Birmingham newspapers there was very little evidence as to which buildings the firm built. All that I knew when I commenced my research was that the firm had built the Grade I Victoria Law Courts in Corporation Street. I was shortly to find out there were many other important and interesting buildings to add to the list. Whilst the architect of a building is relatively easy to ascertain, it is much more difficult to discover who was the builder unless this is recorded on a building plan or been earlier researched. Something that I was determined to conquer.

This meant that every Victorian or Edwardian building was potentially of interest and could not be passed by without an investigation to check if it had a foundation stone.

Asking questions of my first and second cousins and reading the obituaries for John Bowen in the Birmingham papers and having carried out limited research for my earlier book, I had been able to list, some sixty buildings. Intent upon then publishing a comprehensive book describing these buildings and outlining the life of John Bowen, I quickly realised that a building firm which had a life span of just over ninety years must have built many more buildings than I at that time I knew about.

The purpose of this book is to record my further research and to list as many of the buildings that I could establish as having been built by the firm. Even though I must have spent ten years researching the evidence I am more than ever acutely aware that I have only scratched the surface. However, I hope that what I have discovered will assist those researching the Birmingham building trade in those years or are interested in any of the many buildings mentioned.

The result of my research is therefore a list rather than a narrative, a reference book, not a coffee table book. I am proposing to include a full history supported by photographs in a future book updated from time to time on the John Bowen web site – www.johnbowen.org

They two principle building magazines of the day, which were published weekly, were 'The Builder' and 'The Architect'. Both often listed countrywide tenders for buildings which often included Birmingham. Little maths is needed to appreciate that these two magazines published weekly over ninety years results in over nine thousand publications. There was a great deal of reading to do. With kind help, this has resulted in over two hundred buildings being identified as having been built by the firm along with over sixty more which John Bowen tendered for but did not win. This proved not to be such a laborious exercise as I had imagined, and I was a little sorry when we finished after two years. I readily accept that this extended list of buildings can in no way be regarded as conclusive as it only includes those buildings that the architect or possibly John Bowen himself sort to inform the editor. There must be many more yet to be discovered, if I only had time to review the thousands of building plans stored at Birmingham's Archives and Collections.

When John Bowen started his firm in 1870 the Birmingham giant of the trade in those days was John Barnsley & Sons of Edgbaston which built the Council House, the Grand Hotel and the General Hospital. John Barnsley was closely followed by Thomas Rowbotham of Coventry Road Small Heath, which built Birmingham University and Hammersmith Hospital. Benjamin Whitehouse, of Monument Road, Edgbaston, was another local firm which built the Barnsley Hall Asylum; but as the chair of the Building Committee was John Bowen acting in a voluntary capacity it could not have been an easy contract for Benjamin Whitehouse.

Birmingham was not short of builders when John Bowen first started off and the competition must have been fierce. Firms that he soon was to compete with in the early days included Richard Fenwick, James Moffatt, and William Sapcote. It was Sapcote's which became in my day, one of Birmingham's oldest buildings firms gaining the distinction for building many Anglican churches including the apse for Birmingham Cathedral.

None of these larger firms bothered to put in a bid for the first recorded tender that John Bowen submitted in 1877 to build houses in St Paul's Road Balsall Heath, but as the years passed the firm of John Bowen & Sons grew to challenge the existing giants of Birmingham's building trade to become in his day, one of the most well known and successful of them all. All done with acumen, hard work and the sharpening of the pencil.

John Bowen worked with most of the leading architects of his day. These included the London firm of Aston Webb Ingress & Bell, who won the design for the Birmingham Victoria Law Courts; Crouch & Butler who worked closely in the Arts and Craft period with the Bromsgrove Guild, when John Bowen built Aston Board School in Whitehead Road, William Bidlake who designed the Grade I St Agatha's Church in Sparkbrook and my grandfather's home at The Hurst Amesbury Road. Others were, Essex Nicol and Goodman who designed many of Birmingham's city centre offices and shops, George Hine who was the architect for the Asylum built by the firm in Netherne in Surrey, and Osborn & Reading with whom John Bowen must have had a close and friendly relationship as he chose them to design his own house 'Rochford' in Strensham Hill. He worked with many of the smaller local firms such as William Hale and

Sam Cooke of S. N. Cooke & Partners. I am privileged to live in a house designed by Sam Cooke for his widowed mother.

For me it has not been just an interest, but an enormous pleasure, mixed with excitement, to discover that John Bowen had built many of the Birmingham buildings that I know so well, having driven or walked past them as part of my everyday working life in town. It is a great privilege to have a great grandfather who did so much for the built environment that we treasure today. I treasure being able to stand on the very spot that he would have stood upon, and to look up and admire many a terracotta façade.

Whilst it has not been possible to go into detail with regard to any of the buildings listed, it is my hope, that this record with the accompanying schedule will be a valuable resource to those researching Birmingham's Victorian and Edwardian Buildings and those other building firms active in the building trade at that time. Both the Builder and the Architect often listed all the builders who tended for the contract and this gives valuable insight into understanding which firms were active in the trade at that time.

Acknowledgements and Dedication

There have been countless people who have both helped and encouraged me with my research by supplying evidence and photographs of the buildings built by the firm. I very much regret that I cannot mention them all. Those carrying out research on any subject will understand how much a single piece of information can open up avenues of which one is totally unaware. The thrill of receiving an email from someone with details of a previously unknown building built by John Bowen has been and continues to be a constant delight and to whom I shall ever be indebted.

However, I would like to particularly thank Val Hart and Mary Harding. Val for her invaluable support and knowledge of the history of Balsall Heath and Mary for her kindly allowing me to use many of the images from her post card collection. The help of the historical societies of Balsall Heath, Kings Heath and Moseley have been invaluable as has been the kind attention of all the staff at Birmingham Archives and Collections without which I would never have been able to put this book together. Carl Chinn, Andy Foster, Stephen Hartland and the late Chris Upton have similarly been a great resource on many an occasion together with John Lee whose research has expanded my knowledge of the many clients of John Bowen & Sons and established that John Bowen's first wife Sarah Ann Spencer was his cousin and descended from a family of wheelwrights and carpenters. I know how privileged I am to have had such help. All of the above have shown an interest and supported me in a way which I feel both humbled and tremendously encouraged.

It has been a great privilege too to be able to meet and learn first-hand about the firm from a wonderful group of former employees of the firm namely - Maureen Field, John Godrich, Mick Silver and Vic Sutton.

I would also like to thank, Donald Abbot, Josiah English, Christine Midgley and Gill Thomas for assisting me with many hours of reading through The Builder and The Architect magazines. I treasure the memories and fun of finding John Bowen's name listed in a tender. 'Got one'; was the cry in the quiet of Birmingham Library.

Hopefully there will be many more cries of jubilation ahead for those who are researching any of the buildings that we have been able to source as being built by John Bowen & Sons.

John Bowen & Sons

John Bowen was born on the 16 December 1844 in Rochford, a village two and a half miles from Tenbury Wells in Worcestershire. His father Thomas was a blacksmith and ran the Smithy fronting the road in Upper Rochford.

The Bowen family had lived in Rochford for at least four generations, and in the wider area for over two hundred and fifty years, tracing their roots back to 1695. John was the sixth of nine children and with an elder brother likely to go into the business, it must have been pretty clear to him that there would not be room for him in the family blacksmith shop and that he would need to leave home to find other work.

Having attended Tenbury National School in Cross Street, John is named in the 1851 census for Rochford as working as a servant and cowboy at a local farm. Later in 1868 at the age of twenty-three, family history relates that he walked into Birmingham with a sack of tools on his back. In the census of 1871, he is listed as living in digs in Birmingham and described as a house carpenter; but exactly where he learnt his trade is not known. It might have been quite local, either in Rochford, Tenbury or Worcester before he came to Birmingham or in Birmingham itself. The father of his first wife John Spencer was a wheelwright and many of the Spencer family were carpenters and were also originally from Rochford. It is possible that he worked for his future father in law either in Rochford or in Birmingham, as the Spencer family were in town by that time.

Initially John Bowen lived in digs in Latimer Street South near Holloway Head; an area inhabited by a number of Welsh families. On the 24 October 1871 he married his first cousin Sarah Ann Spencer at the local Anglican Parish Church of St Asaph, and the newly married couple moved to live in Tindal Street in Balsall Heath. The following year on the 10 August 1872, a son John George Bowen was born. Tragically Sarah died on the 29 August only a few days later. Their baby son John survived but lived only a year and then he too died on the 11 July 1873. An event sadly not uncommon in those days.

On the 7 May 1874 John Bowen married again, this time to Catherine Julia Townsend. Theirs was thankfully a long and happy marriage, and Kate, as he called her, went on to bear John nine children. Albert, Kate, Arthur, William, Ethel, Florence, Maud, Thomas and Leslie. Three of the boys Albert, Arthur and Tom went into the business, William became a surgeon at Addenbrookes in Cambridge, Maud died at childbirth, and Leslie became a solicitor but was killed in the First World War. Florence was the only one of the four girls to marry.

John Bowen's move to Balsall Heath may have been due to the active building trade and brick works in the area or because his first wife's family lived in Blaney Street (renamed Woodbridge Road) Moseley; perhaps for both reasons. In any event after the birth of his son Albert Ernest, he leased property at 16 Edwardes Street Balsall Heath, where he had his house and adjoining builder's yard. This is likely to have been on the site of a former brickyard dating back to the 1840's. He built a home on this land for the family together with an adjoining builder's yard. His building business was under way by 1875 and it accelerated apace.

It is not clear exactly when John Bowen started off in the building trade. One family story speaks of him working in the coffin trade, when he first came to town in 1868. Whilst the firm's post war letter states that the firm was founded in 1875 many of the obituaries state that he started on his own account in 1870. He clearly had skills and was by that stage described as a 'Carpenter Master'. It is most likely that whilst being an employed carpenter he recognised the profits that could be made by working on his own account and was able to buy a piece of land as a 'spec' build and sell it as a profit before he launched into full time self - employment. At that time, it was usual to take, what is known as a building lease for ninety-nine years, at a low or 'peppercorn' rent, in which the builder as the initial lessee had an obligation to build a property of a certain value. He would then sell the lease on at a profit or create an underlease collecting a larger rent from the under lessee whilst paying a smaller rent to the freeholder.

Although he presumably would also have been able to borrow from the Wesleyan Assurance Company to finance his loans he chose to borrow elsewhere when he took his first lease of land in Edwards Street to start the business. Like most of his competitors John Bowen was a freemason. This was usual and by no means extraordinary, and essential to being accepted as part of the trade at that time.

One of the first buildings believed to have been built by John Bowen is The Red Carriage Bridge, which spans the two pools in Cannon Hill Park. This contract may have been due to the influence of Sir John Holder who lived in a large mansion known as 'Pitmaston' whose grounds adjoined Cannon Hill Park. Sir John also donated land to add to the Park following Louisa Ryland's gift to the City in 1873. John Bowen was later to carry out extensions in 1878 to Sir

John's brewery in Nova Scotia Street and carry out other work for him. Later he was to follow in Sir John's shoes in becoming High Sherriff of Worcestershire in 1916. For the son of a blacksmith to have risen to have become a High Sherriff illustrates just how respected John Bowen must have become; born out presumably by sociability, connections, his general reputation, and success as a quality builder.

Whilst John Bowen had initially started by building villas, he soon concentrated on more prestigious buildings and began winning public contracts to build some of the Board Schools, public baths, factories, and churches.

He could not have arrived in Birmingham at a more opportune time, the building trade was booming. The Elementary Education Act 1870 enabled the building of the board schools many of which John Bowen was later to build in Birmingham, Aston and Kings Norton. Between 1870 and 1902 fifty-two Board Schools were built, and John Bowen is known to have built at least eight and probably a great number more. These include Kings Heath in 1877, Arden Road in 1878, Tindal Street and Highfield both in 1879, an extension to Mary Street in 1883, Upper Highgate in 1887, Sommerville Road in 1893 and Lower Broadway School in Aston in 1899. Most of the board schools were designed by the architects Martin and Chamberlain although interestingly the contracts that were awarded to John Bowen were designed by other architects. Many of these wonderful terracotta buildings are still in use as schools today giving testimony to the quality of their construction.

In 1880 John Bowen bought, for £2,250 the premises in George Street which John Smith junior, and his father before him, had been running as swimming baths. This purchase served him well over the years, providing him with offices and joinery yard. Around the same time in 1883, he moved his family from Edwardes Street to a new and larger family home which he built at the corner of Edgbaston Road and Strensham Hill, naming the new house 'Rochford' after his village home. Never seeming to stop in taking opportunities, he also bought other land in Strensham Hill and Strensham Road building at least ten more houses which he retained as an investment.

Other investments in 1882 were two parcels of land in the Moseley Road which were later to form the site of the Moseley Road Baths. He sold this land in 1894 to the Corporation for the building of the Baths for £2539.19/-.. He must have been disappointed not to have won the tender to build the baths himself. He certainly had the experience, as he had built the Monument Road Baths in 1881. He later went on to build Nechells Baths in 1910 and most likely built others too.

With the firm banking with The London City and Midland Bank (later to become the Midland and now HSBC) it is hardly surprising that the firm built in 1899 the London City and Midland Bank on the corner of Cherry Street and Colmore Row. This was followed by building the banks premises in High Street Sutton Coldfield in 1902, Vyse Street Hockley in 1915, York House Great Charles Street in 1930, and finally in Station Road Dorridge in 1959. Many being designed by the bank's architect T.B. Whinney.

There must have been many contracts for factory buildings and these included the Mozart piano works in Ombersley Road Balsall Heath in 1889, The Perfecta Seamless Tube Factory in Plume Street Aston in 1918 and in 1921 the Solar Works for Chamberlain and Hookham in New Bartholomew Street.

But it was not only schools baths banks and factories that were being built, but churches too, and John Bowen played an active part in the expanding Wesleyan church based in the Moseley Road both as a trustee and generous benefactor. He attended the Wesleyan Church in the Moseley Road which may have been another reason for initially moving to Balsall Heath. Although he did not build that church, he was a trustee of it and played a significant part in extending the circuit of Moseley churches.

The Wesleyan churches built by the firm included the Asbury Memorial Church in Holyhead Road in Handsworth in 1884, the Kings Heath Wesleyan Church in Cambridge Road in 1896, The Hart Memorial Church in Gravelly Hill in 1890, and the Wesleyan Church in Hazelwell Road, Kings Heath in 1910. He did not restrict himself to only building for the Wesleyans. He built the Congregationalists church in Ladypool Road in 1907, and for the Anglicans, the Grade I St Agatha's in the Stratford Road in 1899. For the Catholics he built, St Patrick's in Spring Hill in 1885, St Elizabeth's church and school at Foleshill in Coventry in 1914 and in 1925 and 1939 the Sanctuary and side chapels of St Edward's in Raddlebarn Road. During the turn of the century the Middlemore Homes were active in Birmingham and John Bowen built what was known as 'Receiving Homes' to provide accommodation for homeless children who were taken off the streets and for whom new homes were found in Canada. Homes in this category included The Father Hudson Homes in Coleshill and Nazareth House in Rednal both of which John Bowen had a hand in building.

Nearer to his home in Moseley he built the Moseley and Balsall Heath Institute in 1882, and at the time of his death in 1926 he was not surprisingly its longest member. In and around town he built the Edgbaston Assembly Rooms at Five Ways in 1883, the extension to the Grade I Art School in Cornwall Street in 1891, the Birmingham Meat Market in 1895, and Cornwall Buildings in Newhall Street in 1897.

There are not many parts of Birmingham in which John Bowen has not left his footprint; but in terms of the number of buildings in one part of town, this must unquestionably be in Corporation Street. Following passing of The Artisans' Dwelling Act of 1875, Corporation Street was being cut through to Gosta Green creating huge opportunities both for clearing the site and for the building of impressive department stores and office buildings that were to be built along what was to be known as Joseph Chamberlain's Boulevard.

It was under Joseph Chamberlain's leadership as Mayor that Corporation Street was carved out of the slums to form a new street driven through from New Street to Gosta Green. Work began in 1878 and Chamberlain's new Parisian Boulevard to be known as Corporation Street was opened up as far as Bull Street by 1881, and later extended to Lancaster Circus in 1902. The Improvement Scheme was paid for partly by the sale of leases on the street but due to the economic slump of the early 1880's the buildings beyond the Old Square comprising for the most part public buildings such as the Grade I Victorian Law Courts and across the street the Grade II* Methodist Central Hall both of which John Bowen built. I call these buildings along with the General Hospital in Steelhouse Lane 'The Terracotta Sisters'. The General Hospital was built by John Barnsley & Sons with a tender of £117,888 narrowly beating John Bowen by being £764 cheaper than his bid of £118,652.

Corporation Street must have seemed like one enormous building site in those years with substantial new buildings being built along both sides of the street. The firm built at least twelve sizeable buildings between the years 1886 and 1901 in Corporation Street and the Old Square. These included department stores and two Central Halls for the Wesleyans. The feather in the cap of John Bowen will always be as the builder of the Victoria Law Courts, the foundation stone of which was laid by Queen Victoria on the 23 March 1887 and declared open by the Prince of Wales in 1891. When the law courts were finished, they were reputed to be the finest in the Country. John Bowen would be proud that they are still in use today, but sad that this important building is in such a poor state of repair when it deserves careful repair and maintenance and has the potential of being a tourist attraction. All these buildings demonstrate John Bowen's skill both as a builder and a businessman who was able to win contracts of this size.

At the turn of the century John Bowen's tender of £207,256 won him a huge contract to build Hollymoor Asylum at Northfield which took up the years between 1900 and 1905. Not being content with a contract of this size it is amazing to discover that during this time John Bowen voluntarily served as chairman of the building committee of another large asylum at Barnsley Hall, being built at Bromsgrove by another local builder Benajmin Whitehouse of Edgbaston.

With Hollymoor being completed in 1905, the firm then went on to win the contract to build yet another asylum at Netherne near Croydon between 1905 and 1910 with a tender of £219,797. The management of this contract from Birmingham in the days before electronic communications, must have made huge demands on logistics and a number of the Bowen family were drawn into helping out.

Around that time John Bowen & Sons was building Hockley Post Office in 1911, the Birmingham Repertory Theatre in 1912 which was built in four months working night and day shifts, and an extension to the Queens Hotel at New Street Station in 1914.

It is likely that John Bowen began to retire around the age of 60 in 1904, but it is hard to imagine he took his hand off the wheel. He had built up a company with an enviable reputation and was known as 'Honest John'. Quite the best accolade anyone can have in business.

The limited company of John Bowen & Sons Ltd was formed around the early 1900's, and the firm was then being run by his eldest son Albert Bowen along with his brothers Arthur and Tom. The formation of the limited company was no doubt concurrent with the next generation taking over the firm, but it seems extraordinary to us today that a builder would take on a contract such as the Victoria Law Courts without the protection of limited liability.

As the next generation took over, Albert, or 'Bert', as he was alternately known, was clearly the driving force of the firm and a charismatic character, with what we must assume his father's business acumen. Arthur and Tom would have taken supportive rolls with Arthur being the main stay of making sure the business was financially kept on an even keel. Albert's wife was a Catholic which may have influenced Albert to seek work for the building of Catholic churches. Arthur's wife was the daughter of the minister of Moseley Methodist Church which at that time was on the same Methodist circuit as Cherry Street Chapel in town. Both Arthur and John Bowen later moved to worship with the Anglicans at St Anne's in Park Hill, Moseley.

During his life John Bowen was involved in a great many charitable causes and public duties which included -

- Taking an active interest in the work of the Building Federation. He was President of the Birmingham Master Builders Association in 1884 and held the office for three successive years. In 1894 he occupied the highest position in the trade, as President of the National Federation of Building Trade Employers of Great Britain and Ireland and was re-elected to this position the following year. When the Midland Federation was constituted in 1898 he was elected first President and held the office for two years.

- In April 1880 he was elected a member of the Balsall Heath Local Board. He served on all the committees in turn and officiated as chairman of the Heath Committee. In 1883 he was returned at the head of the poll and was elected as Chairman. In the 1886 election he was returned unopposed after six years valuable services by Balsall Heath ratepayers, but two years later he resigned his seat on the local board because of differences over litigation in which the board were involved.

- He was a member of the Tame and Rea United Drainage Board for two years.

- On the formation of the Worcestershire County Council he was elected as Councillor to the Balsall Heath South Division in January 1889. Having re- joined the Board John Bowen remained a member until the absorption of Balsall Heath under the Greater Birmingham scheme on the 1 October 1881. At that time, he was elected an Alderman for the County of Worcestershire and devoted himself to County Council work in Worcestershire.

- In 1892 his name was added to the Commission of the Peace in Worcestershire on the recommendation of the Earl of Coventry sitting until the annexation at Kings Heath court.

- He was Chairman of the committee of Barnsley Hall Worcestershire County Asylum for 21 years until 1923 and gave advice as to the selection of the site and the construction of the buildings. The builder B. Whitehouse had suggested stone, but John Bowen recommended terracotta reducing the material cost from £9,000 to £8,000. The estimated cost of the building works was £152,000 but the actual costs were £10,000 less and the architect George Hine, said was such a thing never heard of before. John Bowen's supervision of the building of the Barnsley Hall asylum probably won him the contract for the building of Netherne Asylum.

- He was granted his own Coat of Arms in 1916 by the College of Arms and a stained- glass window with the Bowen Arms is included, with those of other High Sheriffs of Worcester, in the Shire Hall in Worcester.

- He occupied the position of High Sheriff of Worcestershire in 1916 - 1917.

- He was a Freemason master of the Fletcher Lodge 1031 and in 1889 subsequently presiding over the Fletcher Royal Arch Chapter. He had the unusual distinction of having occupied both the warden's chairs in the Provincial Grand Lodge of Warwickshire.

- He was actively interested in the Moseley and Balsall Heath Institute serving one year as President. He joined in 1882 and was elected a Vice President in 1893 and was instrumental in obtaining a grant from the Worcestershire County Council of £400 in 1892. He was President from 1916 - 1918 and a trustee from 1896. He was a generous supporter of the Institutes work in which he took an active interest and at the time of his death was the oldest of its 911 members. He was also a member of the Council of Kings Heath and Moseley Institute by virtue of his membership of the Worcestershire County Council.

- He was a generous man. For many years he was interested in Wesleyan Methodism and played a prominent part in the extension of the Methodist circuit of churches. He paid for the cost of the tower and rose window at Cambridge Road Methodist Church Kings Heath. He later attended St Anne's Church, Park Hill, Moseley to which in 1917 he presented the Church with a handsome Lychgate in memory of his year of office as High Sheriff of Worcestershire and in 1922 he gave the beautiful baptistry as a thank offering for a long and happy and successful life. Also, in 1922 he bequeathed to the Birmingham Art Gallery the painting 'Autumn Sunlight' by Dame Laura Knight. Dame Laura was one England's foremost female artists of the twentieth century and the painting was loaned by Birmingham to 10 Downing Street in 2009. On his death he bequeathed £1,250 to the Birmingham General Hospital to endow a bed in memory of his youngest son Leslie Harold Bowen who was killed in France in 1915.

- The Dart periodical on the 24 July 1891 stated 'that there is no more noteworthy example of success among our citizens - a success achieved by sterling integrity, unflagging energy and shrewd business common sense.

- Another newspaper article says of him that he was one of the most prominent figures in the Midland building trade and noted for his long association with the public life of Balsall Heath. He was a self-made man, possessing a genial temperament, and was a considerate employer. It was reported that it was no longer a secret that as a consequence of his popularity, and of the good name he enjoyed in Birmingham, that he was freely spoken of as a successor to then late Liberal M.P. Mr Powell Williams as Member of Parliament for South Birmingham. It was reported that he felt himself, however, unable to give this time and attention which parliamentary work required and was content to pursue his public work in the local sphere in which the paper said that he had rendered such extremely useful service.

Although John Bowen stepped back from active control of the business around the age of sixty four, he nevertheless continued to take a strong interest in the building trade and the modern building methods of the day and took his wife and daughters to New York and Chicago in 1909 sailing on the S.S. Campania, to study the construction of skyscrapers.

The First World War year then followed, and the firm was kept going with government contracts under the direction of his son Albert. After the war the firm was never quite the same, and further deterioration took place after the Second World War. The firm moved out to Knowle and built domestic houses in the area but continued with some notable building projects laying out the grounds for the Hall of Memory site and building the Colonnades in 1923, which are now re located in the Peace Gardens. The Hall of Memory was built by John Bowen's competitor John Barnsley, who headed up the firm with which John Bowen had traditionally competed. It seems appropriate that the work on this site was shared between them, as both had lost sons in the First World War.

After retirement, the climax of John Bowen's life was being installed as High Sheriff of Worcestershire in 1916, Moseley still being within that County at that time. The Bowen Coat of Arms that he had been granted was also something of which he was immensely proud. He incorporated these arms on almost everything from stained glass windows at 'Rochford', to the side panel of his Wolseley Siddeley motor car.

John Bowen and his wife Kate lived to celebrate their golden wedding anniversary in 1924 holding a service at Edgbaston Old Church, before having a party with his family at 'Rochford', and toasting the occasion with a glass of lemonade. His children clubbed together with a gift of an Elkington Rose bowl similar to the lady's trophy at Wimbledon inscribing their names on the base.

All good things and lives come to an end and after an illness with prostate cancer John Bowen died on the 26 April 1926 in his eighty second year. The coach hearse pulled by black horses collected his body from Rochford, and after a service at St Anne's Church in Park Hill, bore his coffin to Brandwood End Cemetery where he was buried in a grave under a marble Celtic cross, to be joined just two years later by his wife's body on the 1 March 1928.

Although he had instructed Alban Buller a fellow Wesleyan, as his solicitor in the early days, his Will was drawn up by the Birmingham firm of A. H. Coley & Tilley. At the time of his death he was Chairman of City Arcades (Birmingham) Ltd, Cornwall Buildings Ltd, Edwin Fletcher and Co., Ltd, Managing Director of the Birmingham and Midland Val de Travers Paving Company Limited, and of course formerly a Chairman of John Bowen and Sons Limited. His estate included shares in Birmingham City Centre property companies, a number of houses in Moseley and farms in Leigh Sinton Worcestershire comprising approximately one thousand acres. His gross estate was valued at £134,027 with personality of £70,077. A not inconsiderable sum in 1926.

The firm of John Bowen & Sons carried on under the leadership of his son Albert Bowen working with his brothers Arthur and Tom. Albert as the eldest son took the lead and seemingly managed the business with a firm hand surviving the depression of the 1930's. Up and till the Second World War the firm built a considerable number of buildings in the centre of town including Edward Grey's department store in Bull Street, and York House in Newhall Street for the Midland Bank in 1930. Later in 1932 Lancaster House was built diagonally opposite from York House at the Newhall Street junction with Great

Charles Street. The Beacon Insurance Building in Hall Green was built in 1937 followed by the London Assurance building in Bennetts Hill in 1938.

Whilst Albert's sons were away in the services during the Second World War the firm was held together carrying out government contracts at various airfields and army camps including Honeybourne, Long Marston, Bicester and Nescliffe. A wide variety of work included the re sheeting of Romney huts used to house aircraft. Other war time work included the building of prefabs in Selly Oak and Northfield in Birmingham some of which are still used as homes today and now have a listed status.

With the war over, Albert became increasingly interested in hunting with the hounds and enjoying his hobby driving coaches.

The firm was continued by Albert's youngest son Patrick Bowen, who had returned from the war. Albert Bowen had now retired and was increasingly enjoying country pursuits, hunting with the hounds and driving a coach and four. Arthur became more interested in music and also retired early. Tom sadly died early from cancer.

The firm continued to rely upon government work together with some useful contracts to build schools in Kitts Green and Weoley Castle. Business had become difficult for John Bowen & Sons and the entrepreneurship of its founder was missing. Whilst Albert Bowen was alive, he had propped up the firm with his guarantees to the bank, but on his death on the 25 January 1963 the bank decided that enough was enough. To the distress of the family, John Bowen & Sons went into administration whilst carrying out various maintenance jobs and a sub contract at Six Ways shopping precinct in Erdington John Bowen & Sons.

Firms such as C. Bryant, John Dallow, & Sons, H. Dare & Son, Robert M. Douglas, G. N. Haden & Sons Ltd, Laing, Sir Alfred McAlpine, J. Moffat & Sons Ltd, John Mowlem & Co, A. Pearce & Sons, Turiff Construction, Whittall, and George Wimpey had come to the fore as John Bowen & Sons lost its way.

John Bowen & Sons is sadly typical of many family businesses which only survive three generations, but the firm has left us with a tangible legacy of many quality and historic buildings which are still in use today which we can still literally look up to and admire. Many of these buildings are being recognised as representing a heritage which we need to preserve as it represents all that is good about the precious built environment of Victorian and Edwardian Birmingham.

The two hundred or so buildings which this book references must only be part of a much larger portfolio which has yet to be discovered. These range from the small to the large. A simple corrugated Wesleyan church in Kings Heath to The Victoria Law Courts or a vast Asylum at Netherne in Surrey ultimately costing over £300,000. References to the sixty or so tenders which are recorded as not having been won by the firm did may assist those researching these building as well as help us to understand how difficult it must have been to win a tender. John Bowen narrowly missed out on building the General Hospital and the Council House extensions and would have greatly regretted not to have built Moseley Baths after selling the land to the Corporation. He might have won the contract for the Park Prewett Asylum in Basingstoke in 1913 which was won by the Birmingham firm of Thomas Rowbotham but the bid was far too high. Personally, I would love to have discovered that John Bowen built the 12 Cherry Street offices which went to J. Parker; a building which my firm occupied in 1973 when I founded my firm of solicitors. Perhaps one day I can discover who built 134 Edmund Street which was designed by Newton & Cheatle for the coal merchants G. J. Eveson in 1897 and which my firm currently occupies as modern offices.

The Birmingham Civic Society kindly honoured him in 2014 when a blue plaque was unveiled at Tindal Street school by the High Sheriffs of Worcester, The West Midlands and Powys. The latter High Sheriff being my brother Philip who was a High Sheriff that year.

John Bowen's life demonstrates what is possible to achieve by hard work, good fortune and honesty. 'Honest John' in name and deed. I am sure that his Christian faith and upbringing as a Wesleyan had a great deal to do with what he was able to achieve and I am proud to be one of his great grandchildren.

Buildings built and tendered for by John Bowen & Sons
The majority of which are evidenced from research of The Builder (1876– 1963) and The Architect (1875– 1940)

Key for source

A	The Architect and Contract Reporter/ The Architect and Building News	JG	John Godrich employee
BSAM	Birmingham School of Art Records	HCB	History of Corporation of Birmingham – C A Vince vol 3
B	The Builder	ILN	Illustrated London News
BAC	Birmingham Archives and Collections	KNBP	Kings Norton Building Plan with BAC
BDG	Birmingham Daily Gazette	KNNBP	Kings Norton and Northfield Plan with BAC
BDM	Birmingham Daily Mail	MB	Midland Bank (now HSBC) archives
BDP	Birmingham Daily Post		
BG	Birmingham Gazette	MEN	Manchester Evening News
BP	Birmingham Post	MS	Mick Silver employee
BBP	Birmingham Building Plan with BAC	SEF	St Elizabeth's Foleshill, Coventry
BED	Evening Dispatch	SBP	Solihull Building Plan
BM	Birmingham Mail	SCBP	Sutton Coldfield Building Plan
BN	Birmingham News	SW	Sutton Webster's 'Bidlake' directory deposited with BAC
BWP	Birmingham Weekly Post	TG	The Graphic
CCGG	Cheltenham Chronicle and Gloucester Graphic	TT	The Times
FC	Florence Camm order book and records Smethwick	VHW	Victoria History of Warwickshire vol 7
FS	Foundation Stone extant	VS	Vick Sutton employee
GEN	Glasgow Evening News	WJB	Will of John Bowen

Key for written histories

AMC	Asbury Memorial Church 1873 – 1973	HGMC	Hall Green Methodist Church
BHB	Steve Beauchampé – Balsall Heath Baths – Pool of Memories	HVLC	Judith Shilston J.P.– History of Victoria Law Courts
		LRCC	B Stokes – History of Ladypool Road Congregational Church
BR	The Birmingham Repertory Theatre	MBHI	Moseley and Balsall Heath Institute 1876 – 1926

- BR
  - C. Cochrane – Shakespeare and the Birmingham Repertory Theatre 1913–1929
  - Bache Mathews – The History of The Birmingham Repertory Theatre 1924
  - T C Kem – The Birmingham Repertory Theatre 1943
  - J C Trewin – The Birmingham Repertory Theatre 1913 – 1963
  - The Rep 100.

MRC	Moseley Road Circuit. History of Hazelwell Methodist Church
NH	Nazareth House

- NH
  - Mary Josephine Giblin (1927) – Stories of Nazareth House
  - The History of the Foundation of Birmingham Nazareth House

SPS	Kay Hay – The History of Somerville Primary School 1894 – 2007
BSA	John Swift – Changing Fortunes. The Birmingham School of Art Building ISBN 1–873352– 57– 3
SMC	Alison Exton – Shirley Methodist Church
TEHS	The Earls High School 1652–2000
CRMC	Cambridge Road Methodist Church Kings Heath
NA	George Frogley and John Welch Netherne Asylum – A pictorial history of Netherne
TH	The Hurst 6 Amesbury Rd

- CRMC
  - The Triumphs of his Grace. History of Cambridge Road Methodist Church 1887–1987
  - Alan J Ratcliffe – The History of The Cambridge Road Methodist Church (church web site)
  - Alan J Ratcliffe – The Church of Christ in every age. Cambridge Road Methodist Church

- TH
  - Country Life 9 April 1910

VBB	Roy Thornton – Victorian Buildings of Birmingham
WH	A brief history of The Wesleyan and General Assurance Society
WH150	One Hundred and Fifty Years of Financial Services of The Wesleyan Assurance Society
HH	History of Hollymoor hospital – Fay Crofts

The dates shown below are approximate dates and may span a number of years

Date	Name	Source
1875	Lease to John Bowen of land Edward Street Balsall Heath. 25 August 1875 – House and joinery workshop. Status: Demolished.	BAC – MS1651
1875	The Red Carriage Bridge, Cannon Hill Park B13 8RD. Architect: Not known. Status: Extant Grade II.	Friends of Cannon Hill Park
1877	Houses in St Paul's Road, Balsall Heath B12 8NG for Mr Webb. Architects: T.C. & J. C. Sharp. Status: Uncertain. £1545.	B 1877 June 9 p595
1877	Kings Heath Board School, High Street, Kings Heath B14. Architect: William Hale. Status – Demolished 1981.	BAC – BCK/ AT/ 1/1/1
1877	Sunday Schools for United Methodist Free Churches, Muntz Street, Small Heath B10 9SN. Architect: George Ingall. Status: Demolished. £1695.	BDG Nov 6 1877 p6 BAC –C63(ACC.2005 / 023) Mins, 1888– 1901 & 1910– 1923
1878	Adderley Primary School, Arden Road, Saltley B8 1DZ. Architect: William Jenkins. Status: Extant in part. £2979	BAC – BCA/AL/1/1/1 1878 Apr 16 Minute 638 p279
1878	Closets and fencing at Adderley School, Arden Road, Saltley, Birmingham B8 1DZ. Architect: William Jenkins. Status: Extant in part.	BAC– BCS/AA/1/1/3
1878	Holders Brewery, Nova Scotia St, Gosta Green B4 – extensions. Architect: William Jenkins. Status: Demolished.	Letter in Albert Bowen's family photo/ scrap book. Holt St. BBP 1878 Jan 1 Number 902 Nova Scotia St BBP 1878 April 8 Number 1055
1879	Tindal Street Board School, Balsall Heath B12 9QS (later enlargements 1883, 1902 and 1933). Architect: George Ingall. Status: Extant. £6356.10.0	BAC – BCK/AT/1/1/1

Date	Name	Source
1879	Highfield Road School, Saltley B8 3QF Birmingham. Architect: William Jenkins. Status: Extant. £2912.	BAC – BCA/AL/1/1/1 1878 Jul 16 Minute 715 p315
1880	17 George Street B12 9RG. Joinery works (5100 sq. ft). Frontage developed 1882. Purchased 6 Oct 1880 for £2150. Architects: Not known.	Deeds to property
1880	Marris & Norton Building, 19– 23 Corporation St B2 4LP. Architect: Not known. Status: Original building may have been destroyed by fire and rebuilt.	JB obit BN 1926 April 24
1881 – 1883	Monument Road Swimming Baths, Ladywood Architect: Martin & Chamberlain. Status: Demolished June 1937. £30,000.	JB obit BP 1926 April 17 p392 BN 1926 April 22 B 1883 Mar 24 p 392 BBP 1881 April 1 Number 2671
1881	Balsall Heath Police Station, Edward Road B12 9LR – Additions. Surveyor: Mr. Henry Row. Status: Extant. £419.	A 1881 Sept 24 p1
1881	Birmingham Provident Dispensary, Sherbourne Road B12. Architect: Bateman & Corser. Status: Demolished. £1100.	BDP 1881 May 21 p9 col 6
1882	Moseley and Balsall Heath Institute, 572– 574 Moseley Road B12 9AA. Architect: William Hale. Status: Extant. £3484 first contract.	MBHI B 1881 Jul 23 p129
1883	Mary Street School B12, Balsall Heath works/ enlargement. Architect: William Hale. Status: Demolished.	BAC – BCK/AT/1/1/5
1883	Edgbaston Assembly Rooms, Hagley Rd and Francis Rd corner B16. Architect: Osborn & Reading. Status: Demolished. £11,200.	A 1884 Aug 30 p142 BAC – MS 3/Box 3/bdl 46 1883– 1886 docs
1883	'Rochford' 1 Strensham Hill, Moseley B13. Home of John Bowen. Architect: Osborn & Reading. Status: Demolished.	Deeds of property with The Family Housing Association

Date	Name	Source
1883 – 1886	Rainhill Asylum Annexe, Rainhill Road, Nutgrove, Lancashire L35. Architect: George Enoch Grayson. Status; Demolished. £115,123.	MEN 1883 03 April p1 GEN 1883 20 June p1
1883	The Dingle, 36 Wake Green Road for James Smith (later Lord Mayor). Architect: Osborn & Reading. Status: Extant.	KNBP 1883 June 18 Number 626
1884	Asbury Memorial Church, 13 Hollyhead Road, Handsworth Birmingham B21 0LA. Architect: Mr. J.L Ball, Corporation St. Status: Extant. £4000.	AMC BDP 1884 July 2 p 5 col 1
1884	'Willoughby' 25 Park Hill, Moseley B13, Walter Clarke. Architect: T. W. F. Newton. Status: Demolished 1982/3. £2497.	A 1884 Dec 6 p2
1884	Shop and six Houses in Priory Rd (now Cromer Rd) B12 QB, Balsall Heath (for Mr Horatio Wood. Architect: Oliver Essex. Status: Extant. £2639.	A 1884 Feb 16 p2 A 1887 April 8 p199
1885	A. R. Dean's, 90– 102 Corporation St B4. Architect: William Jenkins. Status: Demolished.	JB obit. BDP 1885 Oct 13 p6 col 7 BN 1896 April 24
1886	Strensham Rd and Strensham Hill B13 8AG – 2 Houses. Architect: Not known. Status: Extant.	WJB. KNBP 1886 Jan 1 Number 789
1886	Strensham Rd and Strensham Hill B13 8AG – 6 Villas. Architect: William Hale. Status: Extant.	WJB. KNBP 1886 Jan 1 Number 803
1886	Liberty's, Corporation Street B4. Architect: William Hale. Status: Demolished.	BDP 1886 Feb 11 p4 col 6. B 1897 Nov 27 Birmingham article and illustration
1886	Wesleyan Schools, Lime Grove, Balsall Heath B12 8SY. Architect: William Hale. Status: Demolished. £2000.	BDP 1886 Nov 19 p4 col 5
1887	Edgbaston Vestry Hall, Islington Row B15. Architect: Osborn and Reading. Status: Demolished.	BDP– Jan 27 and BDP Jan 28 p4 col 5

Date	Name	Source
1887	'Westcourt' 9 Park Hill, Moseley for James Botteley B13. Architect: Osborn & Reading. Status: Demolished 1980.	KNBP 1887 May 14 Number 901
1887	'Langdale' 48 (now 108), Park Hill Rd B13 8DS for Mrs C. Alabaster. Architect: J. P. Sharp & Co. Status: Extant. £837.	B 1887 Feb 12 p271
1887	Oakley Rd School, Small Heath B10 0AX. Architect: Martin & Chamberlain. Status: Demolished except for house. £10,327.	BAC – SB/B1/1/5
1887	Pattison– Hughes 25 and 27 Corporation St B2 4LS. Architect: Osborn and Reading or Dempster & Heaton. Status: Extant.	JB obit BN 1926 April 22 BN 1896 April 24 BDP 1916 July 1 VBB p35
1887	Upper Highgate St School B12. Architect: Martin & Chamberlain. Status: Demolished. £9897.	BAC – SB/B1/1/5
1887	Victoria Law Courts, 153A Corporation Street B4 6PH. Architects: Aston Webb Ingress and Bell. Status: Extant Grade I. £113,353 13s 4d. (Original accepted tender £78,869). Numerous newspaper articles and draft histories including those stated here.	FS 1887 23 March HVLC ILL– 1887 April 2 A 1891 July 24 p53 HCB p 210 VHW vol 7 pages 45 and 337 TG – 1887 April 2 p342/343 BDP – 1888 Oct 10 BDP – 1889 April 17 BDP – 1891 July 22 TT – 1899 Jul 19 BM – 1890 Dec 7 BWP – 1902 June 28 BP – 1888 Oct 8
1887	Wesleyan Central Hall, Corporation St and Lower Priory B4 6QB. Architect: Osborn & Reading. Status: Demolished.	BP 1887 Sept 9 B 1886 Dec 18 p874 Original foundation stone moved to 1901 Central Hall.

Date	Name	Source
1887 / 1888	Minor works in Clifton Rd, Kings Heath, Mary St, Tindal St Schools. Balsall Heath.	BAC – BCK/1AT/1/1/5 Minutes 3036,3103,3131,3267, 3268,3295 and 3392
1888	Alterations to Holders Gaiety Concert Hall, 88 – 90 Coleshill St B4. Architect: William Jenkins. Status: Demolished	BDP 1888 Jan 5 p5 col 5
1889	Mozart Works Sames Piano Factory (now Islamic Help Charity), 17 – 21 Ombersley Rd/Woodfield Road, Balsall Heath B12 8LR. Architect: Not known. Status: Extant.	Carl Chinn 'Our Brum' Vol 2 p 33
1889	'The Cedars' Calthorpe Road B15 1RX for Mr James Hinks. Architect: Bateman & Bateman. Status: Demolished.	B 1889 Mar 2 p175
1890	'Glen Lyn' 6 (now 128) Park Hill Rd B13 8DS Architect: Not known. Status: Extant.	WJB
1890	Hart Memorial Church, Gravelly Hill B23. Architect: Ingall & Son. Status: Demolished. £90,000.	BDP 1890 Sept 9
1890	'Revesby' 36 Wake Green Rd, Moseley B13 9PE for Mr E Fletcher). Architect: Essex Goodman and Nicol. Status: Extant. £2000.	A 1890 Dec 19 p 381 KNBP 1889 Nov 6 Number 1155
1890	'Lonsdale' 80 Alcester Road B14 for Miss Elizabeth Lillington, Badcock's school. Designer/Builder: John Bowen. Status: Demolished	KNBP 1890 April 2 Number 1210
1890	'Princes Chambers' Corporation Street B2 4RN Architect: Dempster & Heaton. Status: Extant.	JB obit BN 1926 April 24
1891	Block of Shops (The Mart), Alcester Road, Kings Heath B14 for Mr John Collins. Architect: Essex & Nicol. Status: Demolished.	A 1891 May 29 p325 KNBP 1890 Dec 12 Number 1304

Date	Name	Source
1891	Oozells St and Osler St Staircases. Status: staircases demolished. £207 and £59 respectively.	BAC – SB/B1/1/9 p 216 1891 May 7
1891	Birmingham School of Art extension, Cornwall St B3 3BX. Architects: Messrs Martin & Chamberlain. Status: Extant Grade I. £11,697.	SA A 1891 Sept 25 p4 B 1891 May 2 p357
1891	Warwick Road Wesleyan Chapel, Sparkhill B11 1UG. Architect: William Hale. Status: Demolished. £5000.	BDP 1891 July 9 p8 col 5
1892	Strensham Road, Moseley B13 8AG. One Villa. Architect: William Hale. Status: Extant.	KNBP 1892 Feb 22 Number 1476
1892	Strensham Road, Moseley B13 8AG. Two Villas. Architect: William Hale. Status: Extant.	KNBP 1892 Feb 22 Number 1477
1892 / 1894	Police Courts, Corporation Street B4 6PH. Architects: Messrs Aston Webb & Ingress Bell. Status: Extant Grade I. £9835.	A 1892 Mar 25 p11 BDP 1894 Feb 20 col 6
1892	Alterations Clifton Road, Mary St and Tindal St Schools. Architect: Not known. Status: Extant for Clifton Rd and Mary St	BAC – SB/B1/1/9 School Board minutes 1892 July 28 p 550
1892	Billiard Room for 'Rochford' Strensham Hill B13. Architect: A. Reading. Status: Demolished.	KNBP 1892 Feb 2 Number 1475
1893	'Inglewood' Wake Green Rd B13 for N. Reading Alterations and additions. Architect: A Reading. Status: Demolished.	KNBP 1893 Jan 5 Number 1620
1893	Birmingham Kyrie Hall, Sheep Street. Architect: William Bidlake. Status: Demolished. Rebuilt circa 1936. £3835.15s.	B 1897 Feb 20 p 174 BDP 1893 Sept 25 BDP 1893 Sept 27 col 4 Birmingham Faces and Places p 179 SW p41

Date	Name	Source
1893	Somerville Road Board School, Small Heath B10 9EN. Architect: Martin & Chamberlain. Status: Extant. £11,969.	SPS BAC – SB/B1/1/11
1893	Stabling at 'The Dingle' 38 Wake Green Rd/ Cotton Lane B13 9PE. For Mr James Smith (later Lord Mayor). Designer/Builder: John Bowen. Status: Extant.	KNBP 1893 Sept 13 Number 1750
1894	Holders Brewery, Nova Scotia St, Gosta Green B4. Architect: Not known. Status: Demolished.	BDP 1894 June 9
1894	St Patrick's Roman Catholic Church, 106 Dudley Road, Winson Green B18 7QN. Architect: Dempster & Heaton. Status: Extant. £5000.	B1894 May 26 p411 B1895 Nov 16 p363 BBP 1894 Feb 2 Number 9989 BDP 1895 Oct 30 p3 col 7
1894	Bishop Ryder Memorial Church, Gem Street Chancel. Architect: J. C. Chatwin. Status: Demolished 1960.	SW BDP 1893 July 3
1894	Bishop Ryder Church, Gem Street. Repairs and alterations extension. Architect: W. H. Bidlake. Status: Demolished 1960.	SW
1894	Coton Hill Asylum, Stafford Sanitary block and various plumbing works. Engineers: J. E. Willcox & Allen. Status: Demolished 1976. £3597.	B 1894 July 14 p33
1894	Aston Police Courts, Victoria Road B6. Architects: Messrs Mansell & Mansell. Status: Demolished.	B 1894 Sept 29 p227
1894	Manchester Buildings, Messrs Lunt & Co, Old Square B4 6PG. Architect: Essex Nicol & Goodman. Status: Demolished.	A 1894 Sept 21 p185 BP 1926 April 26 JB obit
1894	Duddeston Barracks Buildings and extensions, Great Brook St, Aston B4. Architect: Not known. Status: Demolished. £2140.	A 1894 Apr 27 p13 sup

Date	Name	Source
1894	Moseley Road Methodist Church B12 9AH. Ladies cloak room and lavatory. Designer/Builder: John Bowen. Status: Extant.	BBP 1894 March 21 Number 10615
1894 / 1896	Birmingham Meat Market, Bradford St B12. Architect: Essex Nicol & Goodman. Status; Demolished. £50,000.	A 1894 June 29 p417 B 1895 Aug 3 p88 A 1896 Oct 2 p5 sup BWP 1913 Feb 12
1895	17 George St B12 9RG. Extension of Joinery Shops. Architect: John Bowen. Status: Extant.	BBP 1895 Oct 23 Number 11334
1895	'Pitmaston'. Billiard room, stable block and cow house B13 for Mr. J. C. Holder. Architect: William Jenkins. Status: Demolished.	KNBP 1895 July 22 Number 2095
1895	Shops and cottages, High St Kings Heath for John Bowen (now Asda car park). Architect: Essex Nichol & Goodman. Status: Demolished 1987/1988.	BBP 1895 Dec 3 Number 2196
1895	Wesleyan Assurnace Corporation St B4. Alterations. Architect: Ewen Harper. Status: Demolished.	BBP 1895 May 9 Number 10941a
1896, 1897, 1899	A R Dean, 153– 161 Corporation St B4 6TB (The Pitman Building). Architect: Crouch & Butler. Status: Extant Grade II*	A 1897 Oct 29 JB obit. BN 1896 April 24
1896 / 1898	Cambridge Rd Methodist Church, Kings Heath B13 9UE. Architect: William Hale. Status: Extant. £7244.18.4d.	B 1896 July 4 p15 B 1898 Jan 29 p113 CRMC FS 1896 23 June
1896 / 1897	The Louvre, High St B4. Architect: Essex Nicol & Goodman. Status: Demolished. £20,000.	A 1896 Jan 10 p28 B 1897 July 24 p75
1897	Cornwall Buildings, 43 to 51 Newhall St. B3 3QR. Architect: Essex Nicol & Goodman. Status: Extant Grade II.	JBW
1897	Cycle Factory, 99 Clifton Road B12 8SA for Mr W. H. Fellows. Designer/Builder John Bowen. Status: Demolished.	BBP April 21 1897 Number 12871

Date	Name	Source
1897	17 George St, Balsall Heath B12 9RG. Timber shed and wheelwright's shop. Designer/Builder: John Bowen. Status: Extant.	BBP No 13477 1897 Dec 8
1897	Friends Institute, Moseley Road B12 0DG. Architect: Ewan Harper. Status: Extant Grade II*	JB obit BP 24 April 1926. BAC – SF 1713/1716/1719 BBP 12542 1897 Jan 21
1897	Vectis Lodge, 37 Augustus Rd, Edgbaston. Billiard Room, Morning room and two bedrooms above. Architect: Bateman & Bateman. Status: Demolished.	B 1897 May 29 p484
1898	'The Firs' 34 Richmond Hill Road, Edgbaston B15 3SE. Architect: Ewen Harper. Extant.	BBP 1898 June 15 Number 14034
1898	'Domus', Leigh Sinton Road, Half Key Malvern WR14 1UL. Architect: Not Known. Status: Extant.	WJB
1898	Newton Chambers, New St B2 5EG. Architect: Essex Nicol and Goodman. Status: Extant Grade II.	A 1898 Mar 18 p176 BBP 1898 Jan 14 Number 12583
1898	The Coach House 'Rochford' Strensham Hill, Birmingham B13. Designer/Builder: John Bowen. Status: Demolished.	KNNBP 1898 Nov 3 Number 1
1899	Drains for Charles E Ryder for three houses. The Cottage, Enderby and Ivybank. 73/75 Middleton Hall Road, Northfield B30 1AG.	KNNBP 1899 October 26 Number 537
1899 / 1901	St Agatha's Church, Sparkbrook B11 1QT. Architect: William Bidlake. Status: Extant Grade I. £17,000.	B 1898 Aug 27 p195 B 1899 Feb 18 p175 A 1901 Aug 2 p24 B 1903 Sept 10 p40 B 1905 Aug 12 p84
1899	Broadway Lower School, Whitehead Road, Perry Barr B20 8DP. Architect: Crouch & Butler. Status: Extant Grade II. £19,486.	Aston School Board mins 1891 Nov 1 BAC – BCA/AL/1/1/7
1899	London City & Midland Bank, Temple Row. Architect: T. B. Whinney. Status: Demolished.	HSBC archives UK0009– 0078 1899 Sept 1 p 37– 38

Date	Name	Source
1901	Staniforth Street – rented shed and yard. Status: Demolished.	Corporation Rates book
1900 – 1901	St Agatha's Vicarage, 100 Sampson Rd, Sparkbrook B11 1LD. Architect: W. H. Bidlake. Status: Extant. £2,700.	SW
1901 – 1905	Hollymoor Hospital, Tessal Lane, Northfield B31 5EX. Architect: William Martin. Status: Extant in part (water tower chapel and administration building) Grade II. £207,256.	B 1898 Mar 12 p258 B 1904 Nov 5 p469 BDP 1900 Mar 30 BDP 1900 June 7 p7 col 7. HH FS 1905 6 May
1901 / 1903	Central Hall Corporation St B4 6QB. Architect: Ewen Harper. Status: Extant Grade II* £60/65,000.	BAC – Building contract M6/36 A 1901 Aug 2 p17 DN 1903 Sept 16 p12 DN 1903 Sept 17 p4 col 4 BAC – WH and WH150 BAC – MS 4991 (2020/007)
1901 / 1904	The Wesleyan Assurance Head Office, Steelhouse Lane B4 6AR. Architect: Ewen Harper. Status: Demolished.	BAC – WH 1043425/ LF63.606
1902 / 1904	Theatre Royal, New St. B2. Portland stone facade. Architect: Not known. Status: Demolished.	BWP 1913 Feb 12
1901 / 1902	London City & Midland Bank, 8 High St Sutton Coldfield B72 1XA. Architect: T. B. Whinney. Status: Extant. Locally listed Grade A.	SCBP 1901 20 Aug Number 1165
1902	Woodcock St Baths B4. Architect: Not known. Status: Extant Grade II.	BAC– BCC/1/AL/1
1903	Shirley Wesleyan Church, 257 Stratford Rd B90 3AL. Architect: Not known. Status: Demolished	SMC p5
1903	The Red Lion, Vicarage Road, Kings Heath, B14 7LY. Architect: C. E. Bateman. Status: Extant Grade II.	FC. The Florence Camm windows were installed by John Bowen who may have built the whole building.

Date	Name	Source
1905 – 1908	Netherne Asylum, Coulsdon Surrey CR5. Architect: George H Hine & Co. Status: Extant except water tower. £219,797.	NA FS 1905 18 Oct B 1904 Nov 12 p506 A 1915 Oct 29 p342
1907	Motor house to 'Glen Lyn' 60 (now 128) Park Hill Road, Moseley, Birmingham B13 8DS. Status: Extant.	KNNBP 1907 May 8 Number 2339
1907	Congregational Church. 196 Ladypool Road, Sparkbrook B12 8JS Architect: William Hale. Status: Extant. £2066.	LRCC BBP 1905 Jan 14 Number 19563 (BBP 1905 May 18 Number 19756a is missing)
1908	Birmingham Public Baths. Architect: A Harrison. £15,497.	A 31 Jan 31 p11 sup
1908	The Hurst, 6 Amesbury Rd B13 8LD. Architect: William H. Bidlake. Status: Extant. £3750.	TH. KNNBP 1908 Mar 24 Number 2621 Home of Arthur J Bowen
1909	Additional (laundry chapel and babies' rooms) for St Edwards wing for Rev G V Hudson (Father Hudson Homes) Gerards Way, Coleshill, Birmingham B46 3FG. Architect: Henry T. Sandy Status: Demolished. £2759.	A 1909 July 30 p9 sup
1909	Temporary Chapel for Hazelwell Methodist Church, Vicarage Road, Kings Heath. Wood with corrugated iron roof. Designer/Builder: John Bowen. Status: Demolished	KNNBP 1909 Oct 14 Number 1321 BAC and All Saints Church Kings Heath – Stan Budd Collection
1910	Hazelwell Church, Vicarage Road, Kings Heath. Architect: Ewen Harper. Status: Demolished 1910. £1,550.	MRC
1908 / 1910	Nechells Baths, Nechells Park Rd B7 5PD. Architect: Arthur Harrison. Status: Extant. Grade II. £21,995.	FS 1910 22 June BDG 1913 June 23
1911	Colmore Rd School Kings Heath B. Architect: Ewen Harper & Brothers. Status: Extant. £1,700.	BDG 1911 April 21

Date	Name	Source
1911	Nazareth House, Rednal B45. Architect: Messrs Pugin and Pugin. Status: Demolished. £12,770.	The Generalate Archive of The Congregation of the Sisters of Nazareth. THFBNH – FFK/1/3/1 NH
1911	School for St John and St Martin, Roman Catholic Church, George Rd, Balsall Heath B12 9RG. Architect: Mr. Powell. Status: Extant.	B 1911 May 5 p560
1911	Hockley Post Office, 23 Hockley Hill B18 5AQ. Architect: Edward Cropper. Status: Extant.	National Archives Post Office Works 13– 403
1911	Holbrooks vinegar factory Dartmouth St. Bordesley Extensions. Architect: Pritchard & Pritchard. Status: Demolished.	B 1911 June 30 p825
1912 – 1913	Birmingham Repertory Theatre, Station Street B5 4DY. Architect: S. N. Cooke. Status: Extant. Grade II. £17,000.	BR x 3 BAC – MS978 BWP 1913 Feb 12 BG 1913 Feb 21
1912	St Stephen's Works, St Stephen's St/ Newtown Row B6. Architect: J.P. Osborne. Status: Demolished.	B 1915 Jan 22 p91 BBP 1912 No.32,459
1913	The Britannic Insurance Co. Easy Row/ Broad Street B1. Architect: S. N. Cooke. Status: Demolished.	B 1912 Dec 6 p688 BBP No. 23,075
1914	Birmingham Repertory Theatre, Studio, corner of Dudley and Hinkley Street B5 4DY. Architect: S. N. Cooke. Status: Extant. Grade II. £2,479.	BAC MS 978 Studio Contract
1914	'Lodge Paddocks,' Warings Green Lane, Hockley Heath B94 6BT. House extension. Architect: S. N. Cooke. Status: Extant.	Home of Albert E. Bowen. SBP 1914 Feb 3 Number 1815
1914	Queens Hotel, Station St. Alterations and additions. Architect: Joseph & Smithen. Status: Demolished. £70,000/100,000.	BDM 1913 Apr 25 BG 1914 Feb 13 p5 BED 1914 Feb 13 B 1915 Jan 15

Date	Name	Source
1914	St Elizabeth's Roman Catholic Church, Foleshill, Coventry CV6 5BX. Architect: Arthur Harrison and Geo. Bernard Cox. Status: Extant.	SEF
1914	St Elizabeth's Roman Catholic Schools, Foleshill, Coventry CV6 5BX. Architect: Arthur Harrison and Geo. Bernard Cox. Status: Extant. £4,222.	SEF
1915	The Grand Hotel, Colmore Row B3 2BS. Internal alterations. Architect: Nicol & Nicol. Status: Grade II*	B 1915 Jan 15 p67
1915	Extension to London & City & Midland Bank, 168 Warstone Lane, Hockley B18 6NP. Architect: T. B. Whinney. Status: Extant.	B 1915 Jan 22 p91
1916 / 1917	Newbury's The Old Square B4. Architects: Essex Nicol and Goodman. Status: Demolished.	JB obit – BP 1926 April 17 BDP 1916 May 17
1917	The Lychgate for St Anne's Church, Park Hill, Moseley B13 8 DX. Status: Extant.	JB obit BP 1926 April 17
1918	Perfecta Stainless Tube Factory Plume St, Aston. Architect: Not known. Status: Demolished.	BM 1918 July 29 p1 col 5. Newspaper article recording death of workman on site
1920	Children's Receiving Home, Summer Hill. Additional Buildings. Architects: Ward & Cooke. Status: Demolished. £13,937.	B 28 May 1920 See web site for Former Children's home 1929
1921	Solar Works 21 New Bartholomew St/ Bordesley St B5 5QS (now Latifs) for Messrs Chamberlain & Hookham. Architect: Arthur McKewan. Status: Extant.	B 5 Aug 1921 p169
1922	St Anne's Church Baptistry, Park Hill Rd, Moseley B13 8DX. Architect: Not known. Status: Extant. £1,200.	JB obit BP 24 April 1926
1923	'The Colonnades' including layout for Hall of Memory site (now moved to 'The Peace Garden', Bath Row B15 1LZ. Architects: S.N. Cooke & W.N. Twist. Status: Extant	BAC L22.3 Royal Visits/LH3051 Hall of Memory Souvenir Programme 1925 July 4

Date	Name	Source
1924	Hall Green Methodist Church, 609 Reddings Lane B28 8TE. Architect: Not known. Status: Extant.	HGMC –James Botteley (Wesleyan Trustee with John Bowen) gifted the land for the church
1924	Knowle Offices for John Bowen & Sons, Station Rd B93 0PU (now Greswolde Construction). Architect: John Bowen. Status: Extant.	
1925 / 1926	The Sanctuary and side chapels of St Edwards RC Church, Raddlebarn Road/ Bournbrook Rd, Selly Park B29 7DB. Architects: Messrs Harrison and G. B. Cox. Status: Extant.	St Edward's web site
1927	Warehouse Holloway Head and Marshall Street B1 for Chamberlain King and Jones. Architect: Peacock & Bewlay. Status: Demolished.	A 1927 Sept 16 p480
1927	Insertion at Park Grove – Two Camm Windows Priory Road (now part of Priory Hospital) B5 7UG. Architect: Not known.	
1928	Warehouse in Dalton St B4. Architects: Essex & Goodman. Status: Demolished.	A 1928 Sept 14 p349
1928	Trittiford Rd Wesleyan Church Hall, Yardley Wood B13 0HY. Architect: Crouch Butler & Savage. Status: Extant.	A 1928 Apr 20 p595 BBP 1928 Feb 20 Number 45987
1928	Edward Grey department store (Greys) Bull St B4. Architect: Essex & Goodman. Status: Demolished.	B 26 Oct 1928 p674
1928	Wellington House later renamed St Martin's Bank, 98 Colmore Row/Bennetts Hill B3 2QD. Architects: Essex & Goodman. Status: Extant.	A 1928 Mar 9 p378 B 1928 Oct 26 p674
1929	Barbers Teas. Teaplant house, 28 Pershore St, Birmingham B5. Six storey extension. Architects: Peacock & Bewlay. Status: Demolished.	A 1930 Jan 31 p184 B 1930 Jan 31 p286
1930	York House 38 Great Charles Street B3 3JY. Architect: Crouch Butler and Savage. Status: Extant	B 1930 Feb 7 p210

Date	Name	Source
1930	Smart Brothers, 13 Temple St B2 5BN. Architects: S.N. Cooke. Status: Extant.	B 31 Oct 1930 p765
1930	Shirley Wesleyan Church B90 3AL. Architect: Not known. Status: Demolished. £2279.	SMC p27
1930	General Post Office, Foregate St, Worcester WR1 1DB. Architect: Not known. Status: Extant.	JG
1930	GPO Moseley Telephone Exchange, 149 Alcester Road B13 8LH. Architect: Not known. Status: Extant.	JG
1931	Halesowen Grammar School Extension (now The Earls School), Furnace End B63 3SL (subsidiary company of JB – Alfred Simmonds). Architect: A.T. and Bertram Butler. Status: Extant. £35,000.	MB 1922 June 8 p 184 TEHS p35
1931	Hebrew Assembly Halls and school, St Luke's Road, Highgate B5. Architects: Essex & Goodman. Status: Demolished. £35,000 Est.	B 1931 Jan 16 p649 A 1931 Sept 11 p311
1931	Scottish Widows and Life Assurance Society, 11/12 Bennetts Hill B2 5RS. Architects: Peacock & Bewlay. Status: Extant.	B 1931 June 5 p1039 A 1930 Dec 19 p836
1932 / 1933	Lancaster House, 67 Great Charles St / Newhall St. B3 1NQ. Architects: Essex & Goodman. Status: Extant.	A 1932 Jan 29 p177 B 1932 Jan 29 p248 B 1932 April 1 p596 B 1933 July 14 pages 52,63 and 67 BBP 1931 Aug 8 No 54253 BBP 1931 Aug 12 Number 54268
1932	Offices and showrooms for Patrick Motors, 239 Broad St B1 2HG. Architects: W.G. Warr Status: Extant (now The Figure of Eight public house).	B 1932 16 Sept p 485 B 1932 Nov 25 p 924 BBP 1932 June 24 No 56119 BBP 1932 July 9 No 56193

Date	Name	Source
1933	Tindal Street School alterations. B12 9QS. Architect: H. T. Buckland. Status: Extant. £4,500.	A 1933 Nov 3 p145/146
1934	317 Station Rd and Dorridge B93 8ET and surrounding houses in Station Road. Status: Extant. £1,275.	Deeds of 317 Station Road Dorridge.
1936	41A Bull Street. Birmingham B4 6AF. Reconstruction of premises for Joseph Harris. Architect: Not known. Status: Extant.	B 1a936 Oct 16 p765 BBP 1936 July 11 No 66343 (microfiche)
1935 / 1937	'Pitmaston Court', Goodby Road, Moseley B13 8RJ (Flats for The Ideal Benefit Society). Architects: Beard Bennett & Cooper. Status: Extant.	FS 1935 Sept 7 B 1937 Jan 22 p243
1936	Edward Grey Bull Street B4 Extension. Status: Demolished.	A 1936 Nov 13 p212 BBP 1936 Sept 28 No 64097
1936	Dalton Place – Bottling stores for Mackie & Gladstone. Architect: Not known. Status: Demolished.	B 1936 Nov 6 p918 A. E. Bowen had shares in Mackie & Gladstone
1936 / 1937	Richard Lunt, Old Square B4 (Manchester Buildings). Architect: Essex & Goodman.	A 1936 June 12 p312 A 1937 Feb 5 p190 B 1937 Feb 23 p906 No direct evidence that John Bowen built this but highly likely.
1937	Greystone Cottage, Great Alne, Henley Road, Warwickshire B49 6HR. Extension to the rear.	Home of Arthur John Bowen 1937 – 1967)
1937	Hurst Street garage B5 for Evans & Kitchen. Architect: Peacock & Bewlay. Status: Demolished.	B 1937 Feb 26 p504 B 1937 Mar 5 p555 BBP 1936 June 20 Number 66156
1937	Fitting shop and mess room Mill Road gas pipe depot, Duddeston B8. Architect: Birmingham Town Council. Status: Not known.	B 1937 Aug 20 p345
1937	The Beacon Insurance, 1301 Stratford Road, Hall Green B28 9HH (now Centre Court). Architects: T. Wynne Thomas of Messrs Nicol, Nicol & Thomas. Status: Extant	BP 1937 Nov 3 A 1937 Nov 1 p214 B 1937 Nov 19 p956

Date	Name	Source
1937	Chamberlain King & Jones, 77 Holloway Head B1. Additions to buildings. Architect: Peacock & Bewlay. Status: Demolished.	A 1937 Feb 25 p 282 BBP 1936 Dec 3 No 67541
1937	Verity's Ltd. Long Acre/Plume Street B6. Extensions to premises. Architect: S. N. Cooke. Status: Demolished.	A 1937 May 14 p 206
1938	London Assurance Co. Ltd. Bennetts Hill Extensions. Architect: Not known. Status: Extant	A 1938 Jan 21 p 112 BBP 1937 27 May No 68901
1939	School clinic and child welfare centre, 28 Harborne Lane, Selly Oak B29. Architect: Town Council. Status: Demolished.	B 1939 July 21 p135 BBP 74118 1939 June 8 No 74118
1939	Stores for George J Mason, Warwick Road Knowle B93. Architect: Ewen Harper Brother & Co. Status: Demolished.	B 1939 July 13 p87
1939	9/10 Shadwell St B4. Offices and Warehouse for J. Fairley & Sons. Architect: G I Grantham. Status: Demolished	B 1939 Aug 25 p346 BBP 1938 April 29 No 71405
1939	St Edward's R.C. Church extensions, Raddlebarn Rd/Bournbrook Rd, Selly Park B29 7DB. Architects: Messrs Harrison and G. B. Cox. Status: Extant.	B 1838 Nov 5 p1054 A 1938 Nov 24 p238
1939	Buck & Hickman, 38 Whittall St B4. Additions. Architect: Holland & Hobbiss. Status: Demolished.	B 1939 Oct 6 p540 BBP 1939 June 21 Number 74220
1940	St Edward's R.C. Air Raid Protection, Raddlebarn Road shelters B29 7DB. £424.	B 1940 Apr 5 p425 B 1940 June 14 p708
1945	Brewery Work advertised for bricklayers and labourers for those over 51. Old employees welcomed.	BP 1945 Aug 7 p1 col 7
1946	Temporary Houses for London (M.O.W.) Gibbins Road, Selly Oak (demolished), Coleys Lane Northfield (Extant), Cartland Road and Pineapple Road in Kings Heath (all demolished).	B 1938 Apr 19 p 395 JG

Date	Name	Source
1947 – 1953	Government contracts at Donnington, Long Marston, Honeybourne and Nescliff camps and airfields which included the re sheeting of Romney Huts.	JG
1947– 1953	General Post Offices in Wake Green Road and at Rednall in Bristol Road South were also built during these years.	JG
1948	Rednal Methodist Church, 1655/1685 Bristol Rd, South Rednal B45 9TY. Foundation work.	JG
1949	Miscellaneous Work in Warwickshire London (War Department).	B 1949 Jul 22 p126
1949	Renovation of Telephone Repeater Station Bromsgrove for London Ministry of Works.	B 1949 Jan 7 p29
1949	Building work in Shropshire. London (War Department).	B 1949 Feb 11 p201
1951	Re–sheeting in Gloucestershire for London. (War Department).	B 1951 Mar 23 p438
1951	Re–sheeting in Warwickshire. London (War Department).	B 1951 May 11 p677
1952	Building work Denbighshire. London (War Department).	B 1952 Jan 18 p139
1952	Miscellaneous Work in Leicestershire. London (War Department).	B 1952 Jun 20 p956
1952	Repairs to hutting in Oxfordshire. London (War Department).	B 1952 Aug 22 p283
1953	Building work in Somerset. London (War Department).	B 1953 Jan 16 p147
1953	Miscellaneous Work Leicestershire (maybe Donnington). London (War Department).	B 1953 Apr 10 p584
1953	Roof repairs in Staffordshire. London (War Department).	B 1953 July 24 p159

Date	Name	Source
1953	Building in Staffordshire. London (War Department).	B 1953 Sept 25 p488
1954	Building in Warwickshire. London (War Department).	B 1954 Apr 2 p619
1954	6 houses for The Prison Commission, Somerset Road. London (War Department).	B 1954 June 4 p1009
1954	Drainage repairs in Worcestershire. London (War Department).	B 1954 May 14 p873
1954	Repairs to floors etc in Worcestershire. London (War Department).	B 1954 May 28 p961
1955	Improvements to bridge New booking hall, reinforced stairs and new platforms at Vauxhall and Duddeston Station for British Railways LMR.	B 1955 Oct 7 p629 BDP 1955 Oct 27 p7 Col 8
1956	British Railways LMR. Wages staff amenities Saltley carriage sidings.	B 1956 Sept 21 p519
1957	Motor room and goods lift shaft Monument Lane Goods Depot. British Railways LMR.	B 1957 May 24 p977
1958	Rugby motive power plant. General building work at diesel repair shop at Rugby motive power plant for British Railways.	B 1958 June 27 p201
1958	Automatic telephone exchange. Alcester Road, Moseley, Birmingham (south). Architect: Not known	B 1958 Sept 12 p470
1959	The Dingle Hall of Residence, Cotton Lane. Architect: Not known. Status: Demolished. £85,846.	B 1959 Jan p83
1959	Stockland Green School Secondary Modern School, Slade Road, Erdington B23 7JH. Extensions. Architect: Not known. £7469.	B 1959 Jan 30 p257
1959	Turves Green Boys Secondary Modern School, Northfield B31 4BP. Practical accommodation. Architect: Not known. Status: Demolished. £5907.	B 1959 May 22 p945

Date	Name	Source
1959	Church Road Primary School. Alterations and Additions. Architect: Not known. £11,518.	B 1959 Oct 16 p463 No evidence of location
1959	Midland Bank, 15 Station Approach, Dorridge B93 8JU (now café). Architect: Not known. Status: Extant	VS
1960	Ilmington Road boys' and girls' school Weoley Castle extensions. Architect: Not known. Status: Demolished. £18,497.	B 1960 Jan 15 p161
1960	Kitts Green branch post office, Kitts Green Road B33 9QS. For London (Ministry of Works). Architect: Not known.	B 1960 May 27 p1033 The sorting office on island is extant.
1961	Hunters Hill Open Air School Bromsgrove. Extensions. Architect: Not known Status: Extant. £27,294.	B 1961 Mar 10 p485
1961	St Luke's Church of England Primary School, Belgrave Rd/Pershore Rd junction, Highgate B5. Architect: Not known. Status: Demolished 2019. £59,578.	B 1961 Apr 14 p733
1961	Turves Green Girls secondary modern School extension Northfield B31 4BP. Architect: Not known. Status: Extant (to be demolished 2019). £32,974.	B 1961 Apr 14 p733
1961	'Woodlea', Stockwood Redditch, Stock Green B96 6SX Green. Extension to the house. Home of Patrick Bowen. Architects: Not known. Status: Extant.	VS
	Various repair work over the post war period as described.	
1963	Sub contracts and painting, plumbing and general building work at time of Administration	VS and MS
1963	John Bowen & Sons into administration	

Tenders not won by John Bowen & Sons Ltd

1877. Houses in Oxford Rd, Moseley for Mr Potter. Architects: T. C. & J. C. Sharp. Dowse £1,214 (JB £1,305). B 1877 June 9 p595

1877. Houses in Oxford Rd, Moseley for Mr Fowler. Architects: T C & J C Sharp. Mountford £2,660 (JB £2,843). B 1877 June 9 p595

1879. N. Warwickshire Hunt Kennels. Gascoigne £3663 (JB £4867). B 1879 Apr 12 p413

1881. Schools Brasshouse Lane, Smethwick. Architect: J. P. Sharp & Co. H. Smith & Son £1,322 (JB £1,460). B 1881 April 2 p423

1881. Schools Corbett St, Smethwick. Architect: J. P. Sharp & Co. Jeffery & Son £1,144 (JB £1,350). B 1881 April 2 p423

1881. Schools Slough Lane, Smethwick. Architect: J. P. Sharp & Co. W T Bennett £2,815 (JB £2,450). B 1881 April 2 p423

1881. Lecture Hall, Kings Heath for the committee of Kings Heath and Moseley Institute. Architect: Robert F. Matthews. Taylor (Birmingham) £4860. (JB £4993) A 1881 May 14 p2

1882. Birmingham and Midland Eye Hospital Church Street. W Robinson £14,682 (later this contractor failed) (JB £14,789). B 1882 June 24 p790. B 1883 March 24

1882. Lincolns Inn Cafe, 178 Corporation Street. Architect: W. H. Ward. Horsley £18,444 (JB £20,118). A 1882 July 1 p2. B 1883 Sept 15 p364

1882. Bordesley Park Tavern Alterations and additions. Architect: W. Wykes. Bennett £974 (JB £1,025)A 1882 July 15 p2

1882. Dispensary Ladywood. Architect: Payne & Talbot. W. T. Bennett £2799 (JB £2859). B 1882 July 1 p36

1884. Aston School Board. Erdington Schools – Osborn Rd. Architect: William Henman. W. Bennett £3277 (JB £3595). A.1884 May 10 p2 sup. A.1884 May 24 p346

1884. Pair of Semi– detached Villas. Mayfield Road Moseley0 Architect. Oliver Essex. Whitehouse & Jones £1,163 (JB £1,287). A 1884 Jun 28 p1 supplement

1885. Building Inn, Bromsgrove St Birmingham. Architect: Not known. Builder: Woodward & Smith £2,700 (JB £2,775). A. 1885 Jan 10 p4 sup

1885. Dale End for Mr S Mason. Architect: Oliver Essex. Horsley Bros £3,838 (JB£4,753). A 1885 Aug 1 p175

1886. Baptist Church West Bromwich. Architect: Ingall & Son. Hughes £3,089 (JB £3,349). A 1886 May 21 p9

1886. Workhouse Infirmary, Birmingham. Architect: Mr W. H. Ward. William Robinson £59,353 (JB £72,552). B 1886 Nov 5 p686

1886. Shepley Hills Building Estate, Bromsgrove. House on long drive (No 2). Property of Thomas Worthington. Architect: John G Elgood. Barker & Son £1737.10.0 (JB £2,229). B 1886 April 24 p629

1886. Shepley Hills Building Estate, Bromsgrove. Cottage No 3. Property of Thomas Worthington. Architect: John G Elgood. Horsley Bros £ 770 (JB £995). B 1886 April 24 p629

1887. Two shops, warehouse and offices, corner Cannon St and Little Cannon St for Mr S. Boddington. Architect: J.P. Sharp & Co. Parker £2010 (JB £2237). B 1887 Feb 12 p271

1887. Grenville Chambers 12 Cherry St For Mr W G Grenville. Architect: J P Sharp & Co. J Parker £4,495 (JB £4,949). B 1887 Apr 23 p627. The offices of Anthony Collins Solicitors 1976– 1987

1888. The General Post Office 1 Pinfold Street Birmingham B2 4AA. Architect: Sir Henry Tanner. H. Vickers £54,000 (JB £63,800). A 1888 April 6 p5

1888. Ansells Brewery Alterations and additions. Architect: Inskipp & Mackenzie. W & J Webb £4538 (JB£4857). B 1888 April 28 p310

1888. Midland Flour Mills. For Watson Todd & Co. Architect: Baldie & Tennant. Bissett & Sons £7325 (JB 9232). B1888 June 30 p475

1889. Various buildings at Aston Brewery. A 1889 Nov 8 p2

1890. Chamberlain King & Jones Union St. Architect: Titley & Jones. Status: Demolished. Sapcote £3388 (JB £3556). B 1890 Mar 15 p200

1889. Various works at Aston Brewery for Joseph Ansell. Architect: Messrs Inskipp & Mackenzie. Webb Bros £2877 (JB £2889). A 1889 Nov 8 p2

1890. Additions to water tower Cottage Homes, Shenley Fields, Kings Norton Guardians of the Poor. Surveyor: R Godfrey. Harley & Son Smethwick £246 (JB £297). A 1890 Sept 26 p4

1890. Coffee House and Hotel Station St. For J M Shelley. Architect: J P Sharp. Gowing & Ingram £3498 (JB £3827). B 1890 Jan 4 p17

1890. Ear & Throat Hospital. 105/107 Edmund Street, Birmingham B3. Architect: Jethro Cousins and Peacock

1891. Various school buildings at Worcester Union Workhouse. Architects: Henry Rowe & Sons. J Webb £22429 (JB £ 22,689). A 1891 Aug 14 p8. Worcester Journal 1891 Aug 1 p 3

1893. The Victoria Institute Worcester. Architect: John W Simpson & E J Milner Allen. J Wood Worcester £23,833 (JB £24,065). Worcester Chronicle 1893 Jan 28 A 1893 Jan 27 p14 sup B1893 Jan 28 p15 sup

1892. St Agnes Church Park Hill, Moseley. Nave and Aisle. Architect: William Hale. Bishop & Charles £3600 (JB£3954). A 1892 June 17 p18 sup

1893. Reconstruction of Empire Palace of Varieties for Empire Palace Company Ltd. Architect: Frank Matcham. B Whitehouse £10,875 (JB £11,437). A 1893 Nov 17 p12 B 1893 Nov 18 p383

1894. Electric Light Station Sandy Lane, Coventry. Architect: G & I Steane. C G Hill Coventry £6649 (JB £7597). A 1894 June 29 p13 sup B 1894 June 30 p507

1894. Moseley and Balsall Heath Baths. Architect; William Hale. Status: Extant Grade II* W & J Webb £23,764 (JB £25,337). BHB BP 1884 Jan 3 p3 col 4

1894. The General Hospital Steelhouse Lane. Architect: William Henman. Status: Extant. John Barnsley & Sons £117,888 (JB £118,652). A 1895 Jan 4 p3 A 1894 Mar 23 p13 sup B 1894 March 3 p245

1894. Infirmary Workhouse Erdington for Guardians of Poor. Architect: Cooper Whitwell. Gowing & Ingram £9133 (JB £9997). A 1894 May 4 p15 sup

1894. Additions Queen Mary's School Walsall. Architect: Bailey & McConnal. R M Hughes £3921 (JB £4300). A 1894 Sept 7 p16 sup B 1894 Sept 8 p180

1894. Infirmary at Selly Oak Workhouse. Architect: Daniel Arkell. T Rowbotham £17,987 (JB£19,376). A 1894 Sept 21 p15 sup B 1894 Dec 22 p463

1894. Stafford General Infirmary Various buildings. Architect: Aston Webb. J Gethin of Stafford £9591 (JB £10834). B July 28 p 68

1894. New Cellars Ansells Brewery. Architect: Inskipp & Mackenzie. John Barnsley £ 3088 (JB £3217). B 1894 Sept 8 p423

1895. Mixed School Red Lane Coventry. Architect: Steane. C Garlick £4180 (JB £4888). A 1894 Nov 9 p14 sup

1898. Erdington Cottage Homes. Architect: Franklin Cross and Nicols. W Lee & Son £42,721 (JB £45,779). A 1898 April 8 p10

1898. Moseley School of Art. Architect: William Bidlake. Smith & Pitts £10,247 (JB £10,847). BSAM 1898

1899. Warehouses adjacent to The Hop Market Commercial Hotel Worcester. Architect: H Rowe & Son. Stoke Bros £4827 (JB £5120). B 1899 Feb 17 p15

1899. Wards at Kings Norton Workhouse for Kings Norton Guardians. Architect: C Whitwell & Son. Whitehouse & Sons £5469 (JB £5840). B 1899 Sept 30 p313

1899. Depot and Public Offices Yardley RDC Stratford Rd Sparkhill. Architect: Arthur Harrison. W Bishop Kings Heath £10,687 (JB £11,065). B 1899 Oct 21 p383

1899. Leicester Corporation Wholesale Markets. Architect: Walter Brand. T Herbert of Leicester £32,050 (JB £35,335). B 1899 Nov 18 p477

1900. Ansells Brewery Offices stables and bottle store. Architect: Inskipp & Mackenzie. John Barnsley & Sons £31,888 (JB £33,222). B 1900 Feb 3 p125

1900. Isolation Hospital. Hayley Green Lutley Worcestershire. Architects: (joint) A T Butler and H T Hare. W Willetts Old Hill £9447 (JB 11,079). B 1900 Feb 17 p179

1901. Wolverhampton Exhibition Hall. J Herbert £7297 (JB £8507). A 1901 Oct 4 p 2 sup 2

1902. Slade Rd Board School, Erdington. Architect: William Jenkins. Builder: Thomas Johnson (JB Disputed with Arbitration) BAC – BCAL1112

1905. Hall for Alfred Herbert Engineers Coventry. Architect: Tait & Herbert. Isaac & Son £863 (JB£1191). B 1905 April 15 p421

1908. Schools at Bullholes Bilston. Architect: Bailey & McConnal. H Gough £13,850 (JB£15,555). B 1908 Feb 1 p135

1905. Reformatory School Kenilworth for girls. Architect: C M C Armstrong. C Hope £4912 (JB £5600). B 1905 Sept 30 p354

1906. Union and Nurses Home Selly Oak Infirmary. Architect: C Whitwell & Son. Johnson £3,1937 (JB £35,690). A 1906 Apr 13 p12 sup

1906. Shops and Bakehouse. Architect: Nowell Parr & Kates. R Fenwick £5900 (JB £5900). A 1906 June 1 p11 sup

1906. Tramway Depot Moseley Road. Architect: F B Osborn. Wilcock & Co £24,396 (JB £24,924). A 1906 Jan 5 p8 sup

1907. Birmingham Council House extension First Contract. Architect: H V Ashley & Winton Newman. Rowbotham £25,877 (JB £27646). A 1907 Dec 13 p15 sup

1907. Droitwich Post Office. Griffiths £2583.12.0 (JB £2728). A 1907 18 Jan p11 sup

1908. Aston Generating Station. Surveyor: F W Richardson. Harper £4737.3.6 (JB £5149). A 1907 Mar 27 p10 sup

1908. Solihull Workhouse Administration block. Architect: W H Ward. T & W Thompson £5128 (JB £5797) Architects estimate £5790. A 1907 Apr 3 p11 sup

1909. Handsworth Chapel at the Leverretts. Bishop £5999 (JB £ 6733). A 1909 July 30 p10 sup

1909. Worcester Girls School at the Victoria Institute. Architect: A G Parker. Bowers £6384 (JB £6714). A 1909 Aug 20 p16

1908. Salterley Grange Sanatorium. S F Swift £5984 (JB £7497). CCGG 1908 March 14 p4

1911. Alterations for Warwickshire Royal Horse Artillery, 9 Warwick Place and 9 Clarendon Place Leamington Spa. Architect: F P Trepass & Son. Gathercole Leamington Spa £1536.14.0 (JB £1680). A 1911 June 30 p11 sup

1912. Engine House, Engineers and Blacksmiths shops at Western Road Workhouse . Architect: W H Ward. G Webb & Sons £1121 (JB £1079 – withdrawn). A 1912 May 24 p11 B 1912 May 24 p619

1912. Birmingham Council House Second Extension Contract. Architect: H V Ashley & Winton Newman. J Barnsley & Sons £57,058 (JB £59,134) B 1912 Sept 27 p11

1913. Park Prewett Asylum, Basingstoke. Architect: G H Hine & H Carter Pegg. T Rowbotham £258,777 (JB £290,400). A 1913 Oct 24 p19 sup

1914. House and Cottages at Honiley for Herbert L Wade. Architect: C F Bateman. Bragg Solihull £9805 (JB £14,266). A 1914 Feb 20 p19 sup

1914. House at Honiley for C Wade. Architect: C F Bateman. Bragg Solihull £4514 (JB £5444). A 1914 Feb 20 p17 sup

1924. John Lewis Corporation St. Architect: G de C Fraser & Ainley. W Moss & Sons £215,000 (JB 237,779).

1932. Birmingham Law Society Temple St facing with Portland stone. Architect: R Fenwick (no prices quoted). Status: Extant. 1932 Nov 30 Birmingham Law Society Minutes

The Bowen Family

John Bowen and his wife Catherine Julia Bowen.

The sketch of John Bowen included in The Dart Magazine on 24 July 1891 records the opening of Birmingham's Victoria Law Courts by H.R.H Prince Albert, The Prince of Wales on 21 July 1891, when John Bowen was formerly introduced.

The family group of Arthur John Bowen with his wife Mary Irene Bowen at The Hurst, Amesbury Road, Moseley, possibly following the baptism of Margaret Bowen (the author's mother) in 1912, together with members of the Bowen family.

L to R standing – brother William Henry Bowen, brother Leslie Harold Bowen, sister Florence May Bowen, brother Albert Ernest Bowen, sister Kate Elizabeth Bowen, and brother Thomas Oliver Bowen.

Seated – Arthur John Bowen, son John Hardwick Bowen (aged 6), daughter Irene Joyce Bowen (seated in front aged 3), wife Mary Irene Bowen (with Margaret Bowen the author's mother in her arms), daughter Mary Katherine Bowen (aged 4), May Bagawanath (the fiancee of Thomas Bowen), and Frances Louise Bowen (the wife of Albert Ernest Bowen) with Mary Louise Bowen in her arms.

Examples of Churches, Commercial buildings, Hospitals, Houses, Plant and Equipement and Schools, built by John Bowen & Sons Ltd together with The Victoria Law Courts and The Wesleyan Central Hall both in Corporation Street.

Churches

1884 Asbury Memorial Church, Holyhead Road, Birmingham.
Architect: L. J. Ball of Corporation Street.

1894 St Patrick's Roman Catholic Church, Dudley Road, Birmingham.
Architect: Dempster & Heaton.

1896 Cambridge Road Methodist Church, Kings Heath, Birmingham.
Architect: William Hale. John Bowen paid £500 being the estimated cost of the tower and the stained glass rose window. His wife Catherine Bowen gifted the panels lettering the Ten Commandments, the Lord's Prayer, and the Creed.

1899 St Agatha's Grade 1 Anglican Church, Stratford Road, Sparkbrook, Birmingham.
Architect: William Bidlake.

Commercial and Office Buildings

1886 The Jeavons Buildings occupied by Liberty's Corporation Street, Birmingham. 'The Square Peg', now stands on this site.
Architect: William Hale.

1901 The former Wesleyan Head Office in Colmore Circus, Birmingham.
Architect: Ewen Harper
Photo: The Wesleyan Assurance Society.

1932 Lancaster House, Newhall Street, Birmingham.
Architect: Essex and Goodman
Photo: David Suggitt.

1937 The Beacon Insurance building, 1301 Stratford Road, Hall Green, Birmingham.
Architect: T. Wynne Thomas.

Hospitals

1883 Rainhill Asylum, Lancashire.
The 1000 bed Annexe of which was built by John Bowen & Sons.
Photo: Mary Harding.

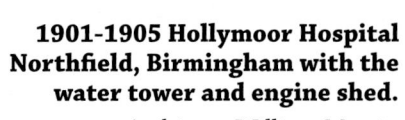

1901-1905 Hollymoor Hospital Northfield, Birmingham with the water tower and engine shed.
Architect: William Martin

1905 – 1908 Netherne Hospital, Coulsdon Surrey. The laying of the foundation stone. (John Bowen fifth fom left).
Architect: George Hine.
Photo: Freda Knight.

The publication of the tender in The Builder 12 November 1904.

NETHERNE.—For the superstructure of the Netherne Asylum, for the Visiting Committee of the Surrey County Council. Messrs. George T. Hine & Co., architects, Westminster. Quantities by Mr. L. A. Francis, 8, John-street, Adelphi, W.C.:—

Knight, Kirk, & Co. .... £266,769 !	J. Howe & Co. ...£238,196
J. Mowlem & Co. 261,539	Holliday & Greenwood ... 233,444
G. Trollope & Sons, and Colls & Sons 258,000	H. Lovatt 229,302
	W. Moss & Sons 226,580
	H. Willcock & Co. 226,260
Holland & Hannen 241,292	C. Wall 223,626
Foster & Dicksee 239,932	J. Bowen & Sons, Birmingham* . 219,797 !
H. Holloway.... 238,565	

Housing

1883 'Rochford', 1 Strensham Hill, Moseley, Birmingham.

The home of John Bowen until his death in 1926. The photograph was taken after the billiard room to the right was built in 1892
Architect: Osborn & Reading.

1898 'The Firs', 34 Richmond Hill Road, Edgbaston.

Architect: Ewen Harper.

1908 The Hurst, 6 Amesbury Road, Moseley, Birmingham.

The home of Arthur John Bowen the son of John Bowen, and the childhood home of the author's mother Margaret Bowen. Country Life included this house in their articles on small country houses on 13 July 1913.
Architect: William Bidlake.

1936 'Pitmaston Court', Goodby Road Moseley, built for The Ideal Benefit Society.

Architects: Beard & Cooper.

Plant and Premises

Office Premises at 17 George Street occupied and developed from 1880 onwards.

The bay window is that of John Bowen's office from which he could monitor the comings and goings in the yard below. Photo: Balsall Heath Historical Society.

One of five Foden's purchased from Foden's of Sandbach for the building of Netherne Hospital Surrey between 1905 – 1910.
Photo: Mary Harding.

Five Foden steam wagons used at Netherne Hospital on site.
Photo: The Road Locomotive Society.

Collecting material from the railway extension to Netherne.
Photo: The Road Locomotive Society.

Schools

1877 Kings Heath Board School, High Street, Kings Heath, Birmingham.
Architect: George Ingall.
Photo: Mary Harding.

1879 Tindal Street Board School, Balsall Heath, Birmingham.

In recognition of the work of John Bowen a blue plaque was awarded by The Birmingham Civic Society in 2014 and is affixed to the school building. Architect: George Ingall. Photo: Mary Harding.

1899 Whitehead Board School, Whitehead Road, Aston Birmingham.
Architect: Essex Goodman and Nicol.

1961 Turves Green Girls School, Turves Green, Birmingham

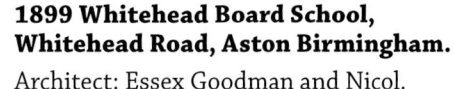

47

Public Buildings

Above:
1875 The Red Carriage Bridge, Cannon Hill Park, Birmingham.

Believed to be the first public building built by John Bowen & Sons. Photo: Mary Harding.

Right:
1881 The Moseley and Balsall Heath Institute, Moseley Road, Balsall Heath, Birmingham.

John Bowen was a founder member, and his children celebrated their coming of age at the Institute. Photo: Mary Harding.

1910 Nechell Baths, Nechells Park Road, Birmingham.

The author was proud to be invited to participate in the cutting of the ribbon to celebrate the completion of the refurbishment in the centenary year of the building in 2010.

1923 The Hall of Memory site was prepared by John Bowen & Sons with the firm building The Colonnades which are now repositioned in the Peace Gardens in Hollyhead, Birmingham. The Hall of Memory was built by John Barnsley & Sons who were competing builders. Both John Bowen and John Barnsley lost a son in WW1 and seemingly shared this contract.

The Terracotta Giants of Corporation Street

The 1887 Victoria Law Courts in Corporation Street Grade 1, designed by Aston Webb Ingress & Bell, facing the 1901 Methodist Central Hall. The foundation stone was laid by Queen Victoria and opened by the Prince and Princess of Wales in 1891, to whom John Bowen was formerly introduced. The building of the Victoria Law Courts was key to the future success and reputation of the firm, but not approved by the stone masons of the day who were understandably not in favour of terracotta.

The Great Hall of The Victoria Law Courts measuring 80 x 40 feet, is embellished with stained glass windows and has buff terracotta supplied by Gibson & Canning of Tamworth.

1901 The Grade 11* Methodist Central Hall, Corporation Street undergoing construction with a Wesleyan Service being held amongst the scaffolding during the laying of the foundation stones. Note the sign board showing Ewen and J.A. Harper as architect and John Bowen & Sons as builders. No hard hats in those days. Photo: Michael Harper.

The foundation stones are shown ready to be positioned. Standing nearest to the camera is John Bowen's fellow Wesleyan trustee Thomas Barnsley, and to his left Ewen Harper the architect, The Reverend Luke Wiseman is immediately behind Thomas Barnsley and John Bowen is to the left of The Rev. Luke Wiseman. Photo: The Methodist Connection and Birmingham Archives & Heritage.

Index of Buildings and other works built by John Bowen & Sons.
This does not include the tenders that the firm did not win.

Asylums

Coton Hill Asylum - Staffordshire 23

Hollymoor Hospital - Northfield 26

Netherne Hospital - Coulsdon, Surrey 27

Rainhill Asylum (Annex) - Nutgrove Lancashire 19

British Railway, War Department and Government contracts

British Railways (Saltley, Monument Lane, Vauxhall and Duddeston & Rugby Station) 35

Government contracts (various airfields) - Donnington, Long Marston, Honeybourne and Nescliffe 34

London War Department Contracts in Denbighshire, Gloucestershire, Shropshire, Staffordshire, Leicestershire Oxfordshire, Somerset and Warwickshire and Worcestershire 34, 35

Commercial - Indexed by name

A R Dean - Corporation Street, Birmingham 19, 24

Barber's Tea - Pershore Street, Birmingham 30

The Beacon Insurance Offices - Stratford Road, Hall Green 32

Birmingham Meat Market - Bradford Street, Birmingham 24

Birmingham Provident Dispensary - Sherborne Road, Balsall Heath 18

Birmingham Repertory Theatre and studio - Station Street, Birmingham 28

Britannic Insurance - Easy Row, Birmingham 28

Bromsgrove Telephone Repeater Station - Bromsgrove 34

Buck & Hickman (additions) - Whittall Street, Birmingham 33

Chamberlain & Hookham Factory - New Bartholomew Street, Bordesley 29

Chamberlain King & Jones - Bath Row, Birmingham 30, 33

Clifton Road Cycle factory - Balsall Heath 24

Cornwall Buildings - Cornwall Street, Birmingham 24

Duddeston (fitting shop, mess room and pipe depot) - Duddeston 32

Duddeston Barracks - Great Brook Street, Aston 23

Edward Grey (department store) - Bull Street, Birmingham 30, 32

Evans & Kitchen - Hurst Street, Birmingham 32

Holders Gaiety Concert Hall - Coleshill Street, Birmingham 21

George J Mason stores - Warwick Road, Knowle 33

Grand Hotel (Internal alterations) - Colmore Row, Birmingham 29

Harborne Lane school clinic and child welfare centre - Selly Oak 33

Hockley Post Office - Hockley Hill, Birmingham 28

Holbrook's vinegar factory (extensions) - Dartmouth Street, Bordesley 28

Holders Brewery - Nova Scotia Street, Gosta Green 17, 23

J. Fairley & Sons (offices and warehouse) - Shadwell Street, Birmingham 33

John Bowen & Sons (Joinery Works 1880) - George Street, Balsall Heath 18

John Bowen & Sons (shopping 1895) - George Street, Balsall Heath 24

John Bowen & Sons (shopping 1897) - George Street, Balsall Heath 25

John Bowen & Sons - Station Road, Knowle, Birmingham 30

Joseph Harris - Bull Street, Birmingham 32

John Bowen & Sons, Kings Heath shops and offices - High Street, Kings Heath 24

Kitts Green Branch Post Office - Kitts Green Road, Birmingham 36

Lancaster House - Great Charles Street/Newhall Street Birmingham 31

Liberty's Department Store - Corporation Street Birmingham 19

London Assurance Co Ltd - Bennetts Hill, Birmingham 33

London City & Midland Bank - Temple Row, Birmingham 25

London City & Midland Bank (extensions) - Warstone Lane, Hockley 29

London City & Midland Bank - High Street, Sutton Coldfield 26

The Louvre - High Street, Birmingham 24

Mackie & Gladstone (bottling plant) - Dalton Street, Birmingham 32

Manchester Buildings - Old Square, Birmingham 23

Marris & Norton - Corporation Street, Birmingham 18

The Mart - High Street, Kings Heath 21

Martin's Bank - Colmore Row, Birmingham 30

Midland Bank - Station Approach, Dorridge 36

Moseley Telephone Exchange - Alcester Road, Moseley 31

Mozart Piano Works - Ombersley Road, Balsall Heath 21

Newbury's - Old Square, Birmingham 29

Newton Chambers - New Street, Birmingham 25

Pattisons-Hughes - Corporation Street, Birmingham 20

Patrick Motors showroom - Broad Street, Birmingham 31

Perfecta Stainless Steel factory - Plume Street, Aston 29

Police Courts - Corporation Street, Birmingham 22

Princess Chambers - Corporation Street, Birmingham 21

The Priory (windows) - Priory Road, Edgbaston 30

The Queens Hotel (extension) - Station Street, Birmingham 28

The Red Lion (windows) - Vicarage Road, Kings Heath 26

Messrs Richard Lunt & Co - Old Square, Birmingham 32

St Stephen's works - St Stephen's Street, Newtown 28

Scottish Widows and Life Assurance - Bennetts Hill, Birmingham 31

Smart Brothers - Temple Street, Birmingham 31

Theatre Royal facade - New Street, Birmingham 26

Verity's (extensions) - Long Acre/Plume Street, Nechells 33

Wake Green Road Post Offices - Moseley 34

The Wesleyan Assurance (office alterations) - Corporation Street, Birmingham 24

The Wesleyan Assurance Head Office - Steelhouse Lane, Birmingham 26

Woodcock Street Baths - Birmingham 26

Worcester General Post Office - Foregate Street, Worcester 31

York House - Great Charles Street/Newhall Street, Birmingham 30

Domestic - indexed by road or street

Alcester Road (Lonsdale) Moseley 21

Amesbury Road (The Hurst) - Moseley 27

Augustus Road (Vectis Lodge) (Billiard and Morning Room and two bedrooms - Edgbaston 25

Calthorpe Road (The Cedars) - Edgbaston 21

Cannon Hill (Pitmaston) (billiard room stable block and cow house) - Moseley 24

Cartland Road (prefabricated houses) - Kings Heath 33

Cromer Road (formerly Priory Road) - Balsall Heath 19

Coleys Lane (prefabricated houses) - Northfield 33

Cotton Road (The Dingle Hall of Residence) - Moseley 35

Edward Street (John Bowen's house) - Balsall Heath 17

Gibbins Road (prefabricated houses) - Selly Oak 33

Goodby Road (Flats for The Ideal Benefit Society - Moseley 32

Henley Road (Greystone Cottage) - Great Alne, Warwickshire 32

Leigh Sinton Road (Domus) - Half Key Malvern 25

Middleton Road (Drains for The Cottage, Enderby and Ivybank) - Northfield 25

Park Hill (now 128) (Glen Lyn) - Moseley 21

Park Hill (motor House to Glen Lyn) - Moseley 27

Park Hill (Westcourt) - Moseley 20

Park Hill (Willoughby) - Moseley 19

Park Hill (Langdale) - Moseley 20

Pineapple Road (prefabricated houses) - Kings Heath 33

Priory Road (now Cromer Road) (six houses) - Moseley 19

Richmond Hill Road (The Firs) - Edgbaston 25

St Paul's Road (houses) - Balsall Heath 17

Station Road (houses) - Dorridge 32

Stocks Green (extensions to 'Woodlea') - Stocks Green 36

Strensham Hill (Rochford) - Moseley 18

Strensham Hill (billiard room) - Moseley 22

Strensham Road (coach house) - Moseley 25

Strensham Road - Moseley 19, 22

Wake Green Road (Inglewood) (Alterations and additions) - Moseley 22

Wake Green Road (The Dingle 1883) - Moseley 19

Wake Green Road (The Dingle stabling 1893) - Moseley 23

Wake Green Road (Revesby) - Moseley 21

Warings Green Lane (Lodge Paddocks) - Earlswood 28

Public - indexed by name

Balsall Heath Police Station - Edward Road, Balsall Heath 18

Birmingham Public Baths 27

Birmingham School of Art - Cornwall Street, Birmingham 22

Cannon Hill Park, The Red Carriage bridge - Cannon Hill Park 17

Colonnades - The Peace Gardens, Holloway Head, Bath Row, Birmingham 29

Edgbaston Assembly Rooms - Francis Road/Hagley Road, Birmingham 18

Friends Institute Moseley Road - Balsall Heath 25

Kyrie Hall - Sheep Street, Birmingham 22

Monument Road Swimming Baths - Ladywood 18

Moseley and Balsall Heath Institute - Moseley Road, Balsall Heath 18

Nechells Baths - Nechells Park Road, Birmingham 27

Police Courts - Victoria Road, Aston, Birmingham 23

Victoria Law Courts - Corporation Street, Birmingham 20

Religious - (Churches, Church Schools and Children's Receiving Homes) - indexed by name

Asbury Memorial Church - Holyhead Road, Handsworth 19

Bishop Ryder Church - Gem Street, Birmingham 23

Bristol Road South Methodist Church (foundation work) - Rednal 34

Cambridge Road Methodist Church - Cambridge Road, Kings Heath 24

Edgbaston Vestry Hall - Islington Row, Edgbaston 19

Hall Green Methodist Church - Hall Green Birmingham 30

The Hart Memorial Church - Gravelly Hill, Birmingham 21

Father Hudson Homes - Gerards Way Coleshill 27

Hall Green Methodist Church - Readings Lane, Hall Green 30

Hebrew Assembly Halls and School - St Luke's Road, Highgate 31

Ladypool Road Congregational Church - Ladypool Road, Sparkbrook 27

Nazareth House - Bristol Road South, Rednal 28

St John and St George School - George Street Balsall Heath 28

St Patrick's Roman Catholic Church - Dudley Road, Winson Green 23

Muntz Street Sunday Schools - Muntz Street, Balsall Heath 17

Moseley Road Methodist Church - Moseley 24

St Agatha's Vicarage - Sampson Road, Sparkbrook 26

St Agatha's Church - Stratford Road, Sparkbrook 25

St Anne's Church Lychgate - Park Hill, Moseley 29

St Anne's Church Baptistry - Park Hill, Moseley 29

St Edward's - Raddlebarn Road, Selly Park 30, 33

St Elizabeth's Roman Catholic Church - St Elizabeth Road, Foleshill, Coventry 29

Shirley Wesleyan Church Stratford Road, Shirley 26, 31

Summer Hill Children's Receiving Home - Summer Hill, Birmingham 29

Trittiford Road Methodist Church - Trittiford Road, Yardley Wood 30

Hazelwell Church - Vicarage Road, Kings Heath 27

Warwick Road Wesleyan Chapel - Warwick Road, Sparkbrook 22

Wesleyan Central Hall (1887 - Corporation Street, Birmingham 20

Wesleyan Central Hall (1901) - Corporation Street, Birmingham 26

Wesleyan Schools - Lime Grove, Balsall Heath 19

Schools - indexed by name

Adderley Street School - Saltley 17

Church Road Primary School (alterations and Additions) - location uncertain 36

Clifton Road School Balsall Heath (minor works 1887/88) 21

Clifton Road School (alterations 1892) - Balsall Heath 22

Colmore Road School - Kings Heath 27

Halesowen Grammar School (The Earls School) - Furnace End, Halesowen 31

Highfield Road School - Saltley 18

Hunters Hill Open Air School (extensions) - Bromsgrove 36

Illmington Road Boys School - Weoley Castle 36

Kings Heath School - High Street, Kings Heath 17, 21

Mary Street School Balsall Heath 18

Mary Street School Balsall Heath (minor works 1887/88) 21

Mary Street School (alterations 1892) - Balsall Heath 22

Oakley Road School - Small Heath 20

St Luke's Church of England Primary School - Highgate 36

Somerville Road School - Small Heath 23

St Elizabeth's Roman Catholic School - St Elizabeth Road, Foleshill, Coventry 29

Stockland Green Secondary Modern School - Stockland Green 35

Tindal Street School - Balsall Heath 17, 21, 22, 32

Turves Green Boys Secondary Modern School - Northfield 35

Turves Green Girls Secondary Modern School (extension) - Northfield 36

Upper Highgate School - Highgate 20

Oozells Street School (staircases) - Birmingham 22

Osler Street School (staircases) - Ladywood 22

Whitehead Road (Broadway Lower School) - Perry Barr 25

Acknowledgement of Appreciation.

I would like to record my sincere thanks and appreciation to Wesleyan Assurance Society for sponsoring the publication of this book.

Not only was John Bowen a member and trustee of the Wesleyan Church in the Moseley Road in the early nineteenth century, but as a trustee of the Church active in working with the then Managing Director of the Wesleyan Assurance Society, Richard Aldington Hunt in promoting and funding the extension of the Wesleyan Church circuits in Kings Heath, Hazelwell, Hall Green and Shirley.

John Bowen & Sons built many buildings directly connected with the Wesleyan Church not least the first Wesleyan Central Hall built in New Street in 1887 to accommodate a congregation of one thousand. After ten years this proved too small for the Wesleyans, and so in 1901 the firm built the Central Hall that we know today which had a seating capacity of 2,500. It is this building that the Wesleyan Assurance Society would hold its Annual General Meetings

That same year that the new Central Hall was being built, John Bowen & Sons were building the Wesleyan Head Office in Colmore Square. Although sadly the building is no longer standing, Wesleyan Assurance Society now occupy another iconic building in Birmingham. They have stood strong in an ever-changing and often challenging world, surviving two world wars, global depressions, and the financial crisis of 2008.

Wesleyan's generous sponsorship of this book evidences their ongoing commitment to the heritage of our great City, and I am most grateful.

Anthony Collins

anthonyrcollins@btinternet.com